Platonic Solids & Sacred Geometry Coloring Book for Adults

Jose Valladares

Volume 1

Intentionally left blank

Contents

Introduction 1
Activity 1: Genesis 3
Activity 2: Flower 5
Activity 3: Egyptology 7
Activity 4: Master Mason 9
Activity 5: Earth Energy 11
Activity 6: Knight Templar 13
Activity 7: Point in Circle 15
Activity 8: Garbhagrha 17
Activity 9: Garden of Jupiter 19
Activity 10: Haiden 21
Activity 11: Gateway to Shinto 23
Activity 12: Secret of Taoism 25
Activity 13: Zhang 27
Activity 14: Seed of Life 29
Activity 15: Star 31
Activity 16: Triangulation Theory 33
Activity 17: Saint Germain 35
Activity 18: Secret of Nature 37
Activity 19: Vulgate Cycle 39
Activity 20: Electricity & Magnetism 41
Activity 21: Dragon's Nest 43
Activity 22: Perfect Symmetry 45
Activity 23: Autumn 47
Activity 24: Network of Paths 49
Activity 25: Renaissance 51
Activity 26: Twilight of the stars 53
Activity 27: Wexicity 55
Activity 28: Mannikka 57
Activity 29: Derivatives of x^2 59
Activity 30: Devereux 61
Activity 31: Chains 63
Activity 32: Glastonbury Secret 65
Activity 33: Eye of Providence 67
Activity 34: Godfrey de Bouillon 69
Activity 35: Shingon 71
Activity 36: Point of Symmetry 73
Activity 37: Peristyle Garden 75
Activity 38: Curatola's last painting 77
Activity 39: Circle of Love 79
Activity 40: Mouse trap 81
Activity 41: Hydrogen Molecule 83
Activity 42: Infinity + 1 85
Activity 43: Order of 6 87
Activity 44: Lost Symbol 89
Activity 45: Triforce 91
Activity 46: Frequency 528Hz 93
Activity 47: Minoan temple 95

Activity 48: Flowery doodle *97*
Activity 49: Ant's world *99*
Activity 50: Universe *101*
Activity 51: Aztec Calendar *103*
Activity 52: Alien messege *105*
Activity 53: Celestial *107*
Activity 54: Arc Reactor *109*
Activity 55: Complexity *111*
Activity 56: Free Energy *113*
Activity 57: Electron reactor *115*
Activity 58: Musical colors *117*
Activity 59: Arcade *119*
Activity 60: Spiritual path *121*
Activity 61: Alpha centauri *123*
Activity 62: Key to Lothlorien *125*
Activity 63: Path to Nirvana *127*
Activity 64: Spider web *129*
Activity 65: Heavenly light *131*
Activity 66: Theta - phi *133*
Activity 67: Cathedral *135*
Activity 68: Pastoral symphony *137*
Activity 69: Hare Krishna *139*
Activity 70: Centripetal force *141*
Activity 71: Circlesquare *143*
Activity 72: Milk & Cookies *145*
Activity 73: Golden rule *147*
Activity 74: Continuity *149*
Activity 75: Connections *151*
Activity 76: Two lovers *153*
Activity 77: Ice crystals *155*
Activity 78: Point of no return *157*
Activity 79: Fountain *159*
Activity 80: Patience *161*
Activity 81: Imperfect triangle *163*
Activity 82: God *165*
Activity 83: Pond *167*
Activity 84: Electrotechnical *169*
Activity 85: Star circumference *171*
Activity 86: Holy of Holies *173*
Activity 87: Atom of peace *175*
Activity 88: Roses of love *177*
Activity 89: Perfect beauty *179*
Activity 90: Endogendo *181*
Activity 91: Melindano *183*
Activity 92: Hologram *185*
Activity 93: Multiverse theory *187*
Activity 94: Seed multiplication *189*
Activity 95: Square in circle *191*
Activity 96: Falling leaves *193*
Activity 97: Polygon *195*

Activity 98: Endogendo *197*
Activity 99: Sacred leaves *199*
Activity 100: Bells *201*
Activity 101: Nebula *203*
Acknowledgement *205*

Intentionally left blank

Introduction

This is a coloring book for a special kind of geometry that is common in flowers, fruits, molecules, stars, and ice crystals, it is called sacred geometry. The ancient Greeks studied symmetric patterns, and symbols extensively. Plato wrote about these patterns in the dialogue Timaeus c.360 B.C, the Platonic solids. Plato believed a cube, tetrahedron, octahedron, dodecahedron, and Icosahedron are associated with four elements, and these four elements define our world.

This coloring book is for adults who want to explore their creative abilities to color complex sacred Geometry designs and Platonic solids. The perfect book for stressed-out adults, who want to spend time with the self. Explore 101 unique sacred Geometry, Platonic solids, and fractal designs.

Tools:

You can color using crayons, colored pensils, marker pens, and watercolor pencils.

Activity 1: Genesis

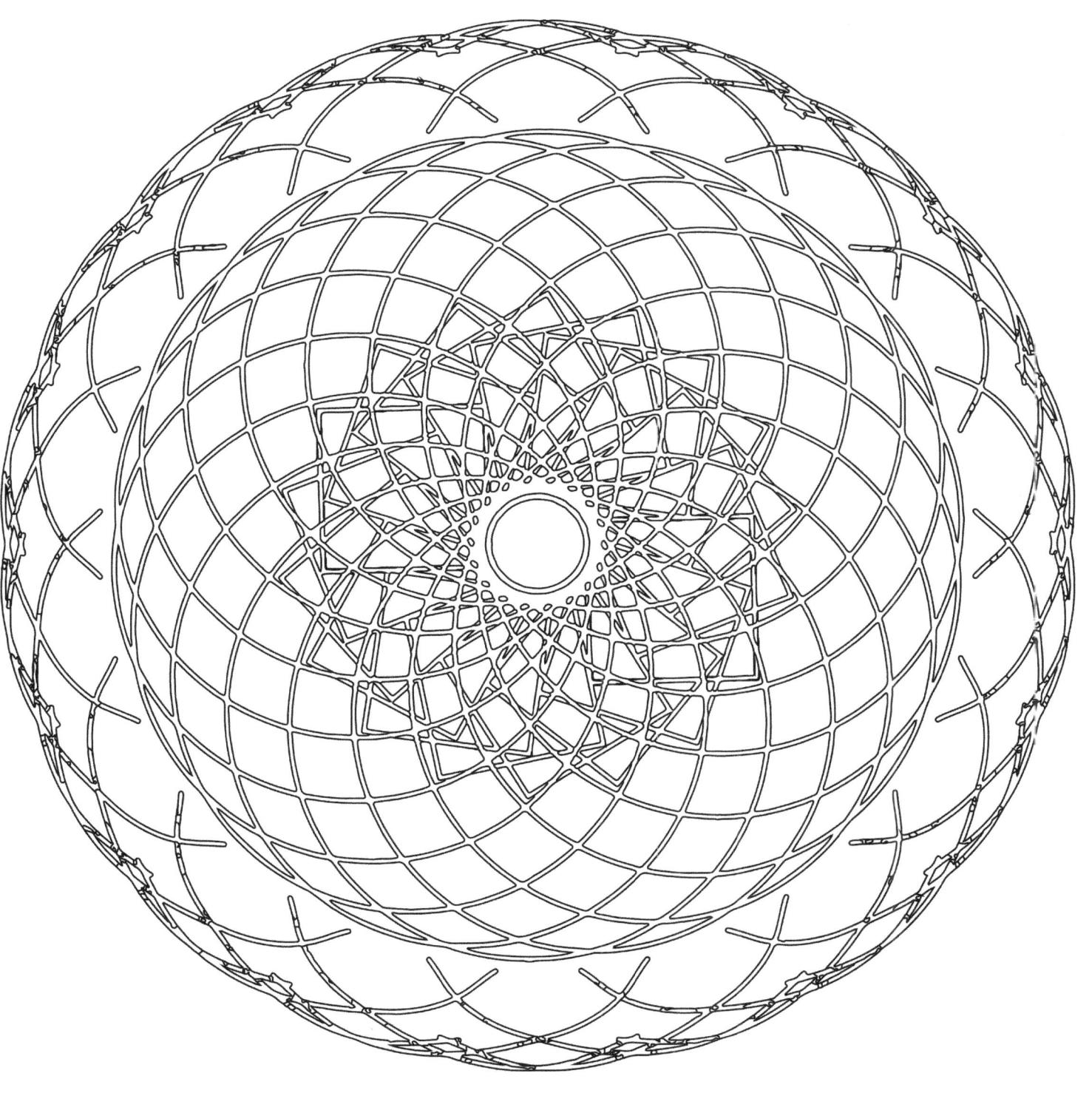

Activity 2: Flower

Activity 3: Egyptology

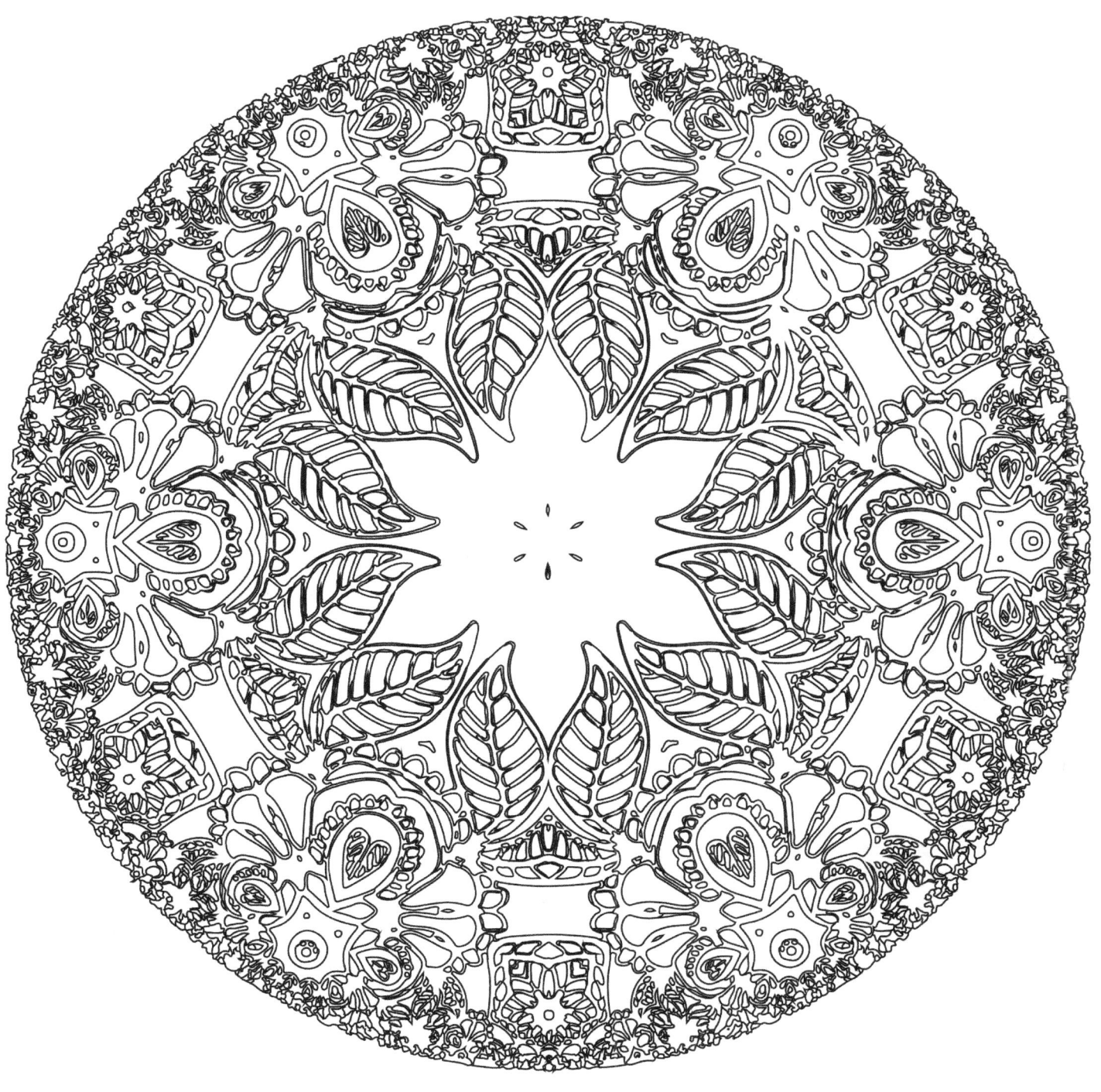

Activity 4: Master Mason

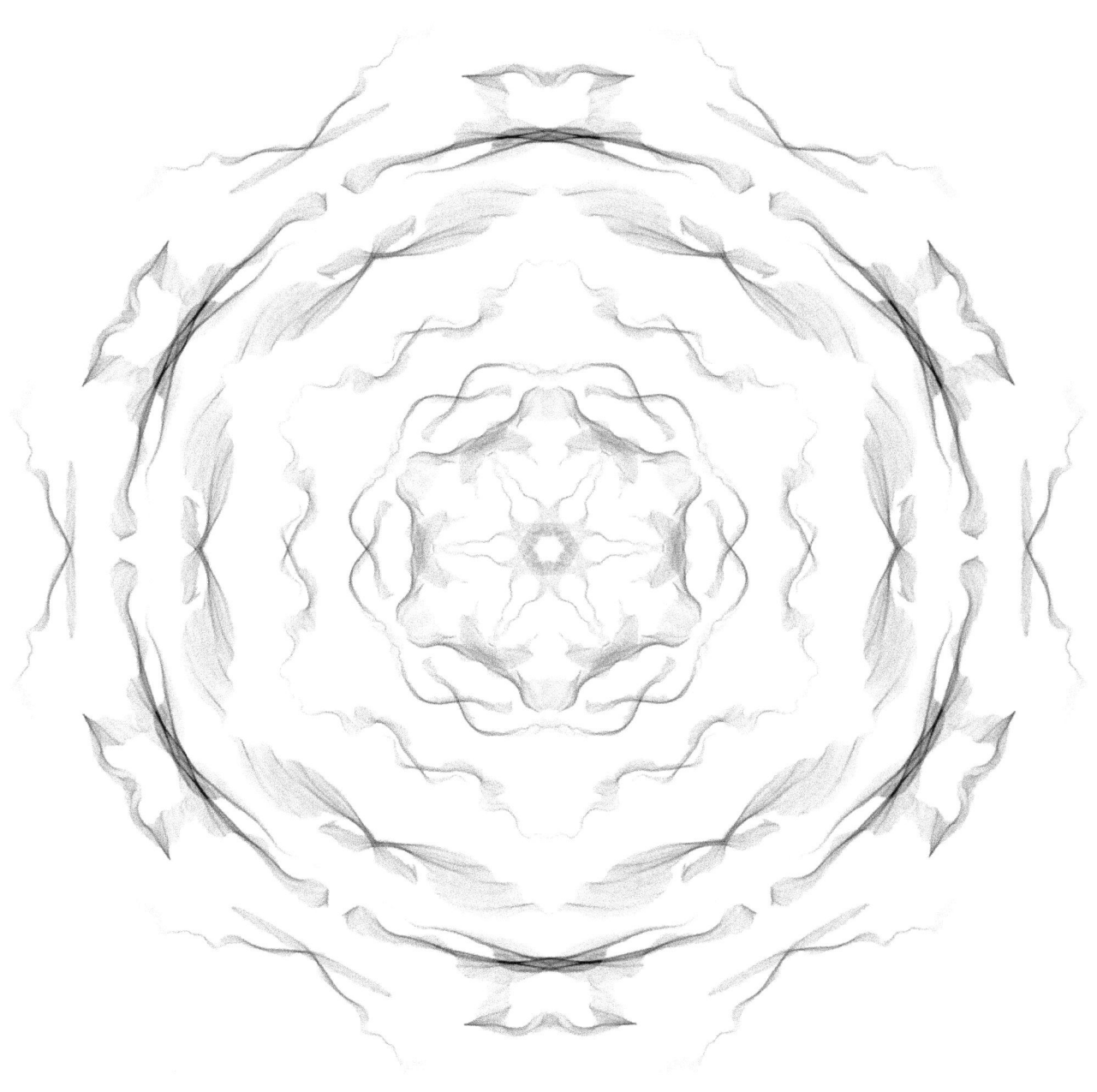

Activity 5: Earth Energy

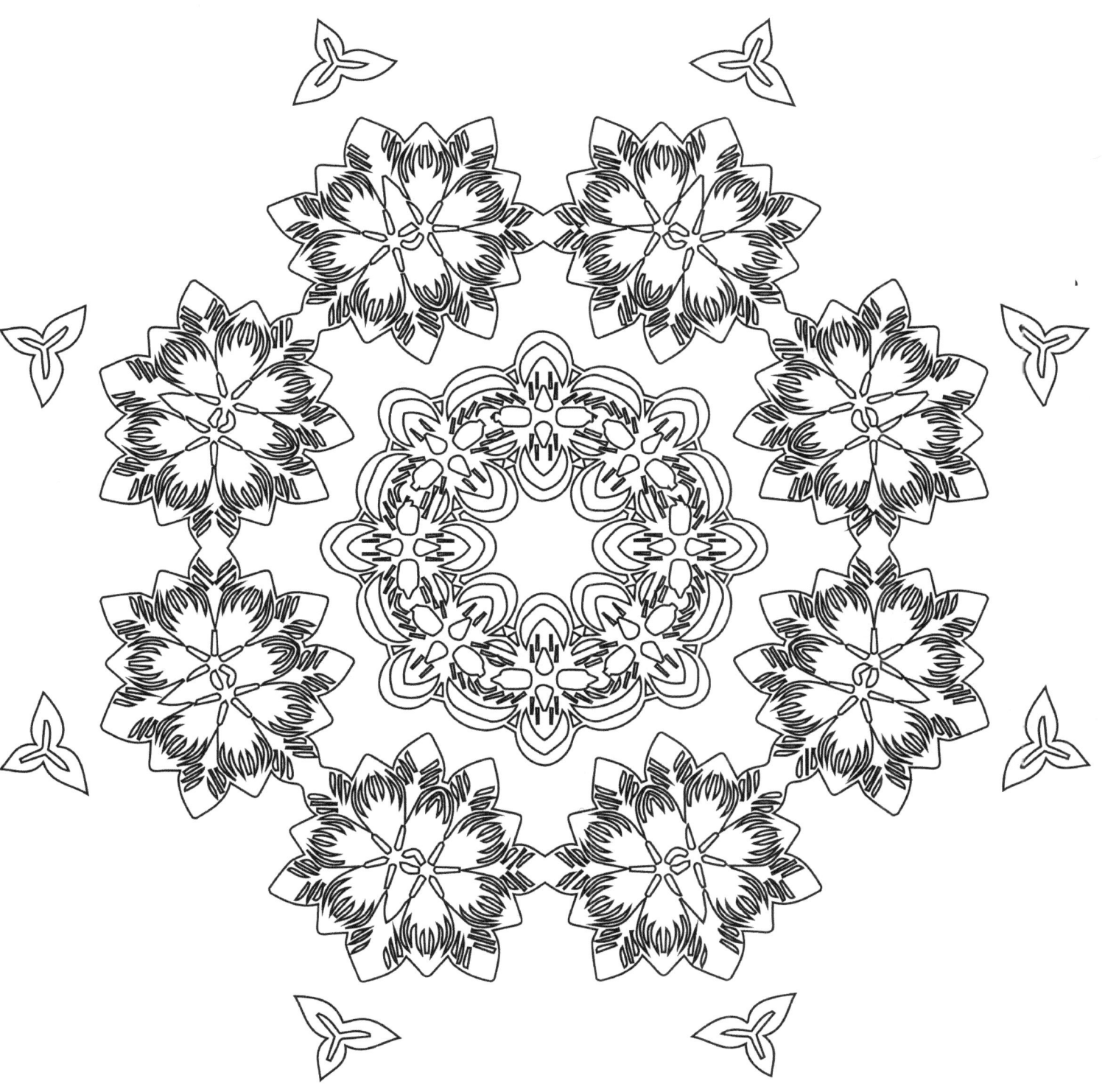

Activity 6: Knight Templar

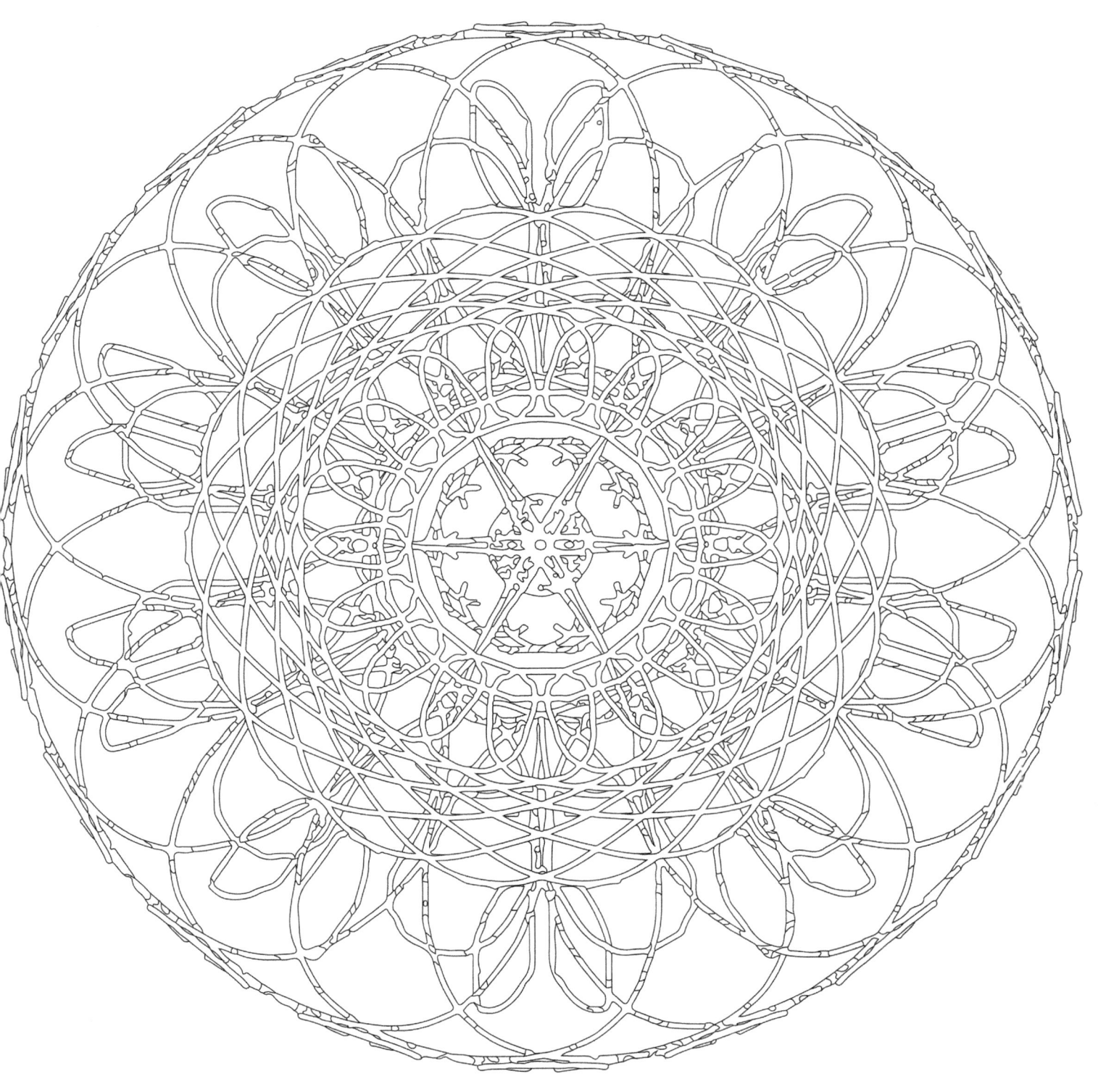

Activity 7: Point in Circle

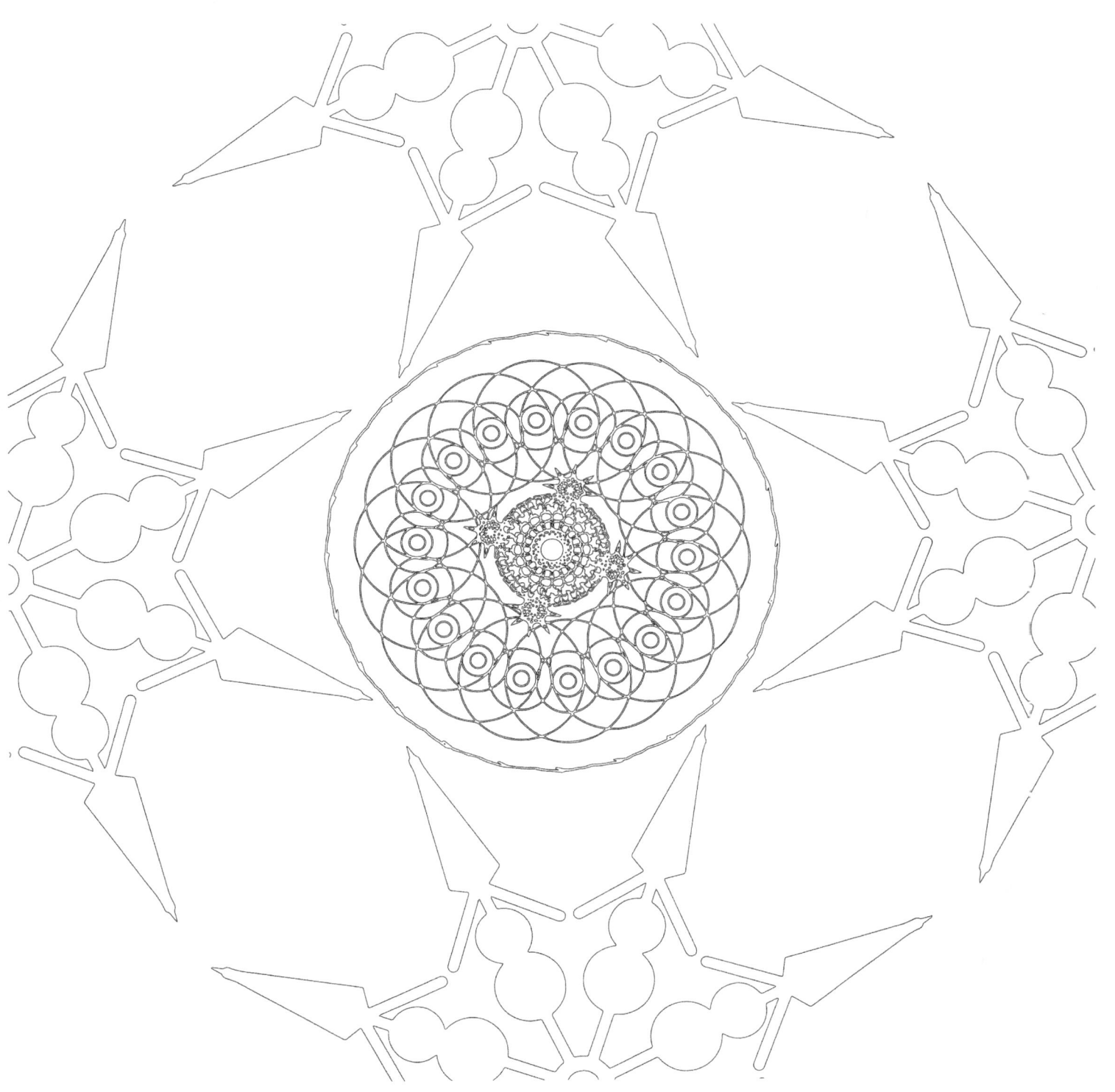

Activity 8: Garbhagrha

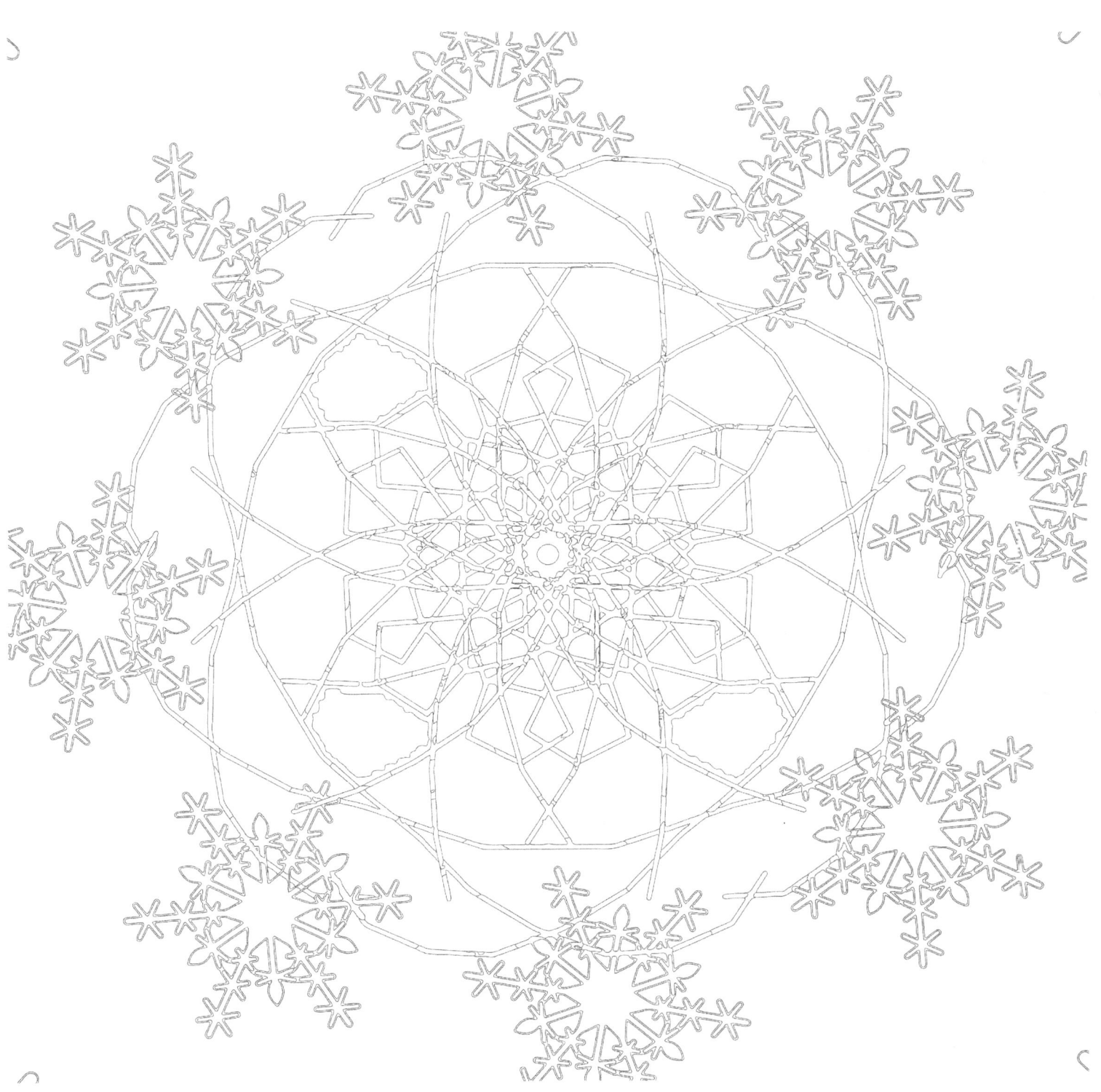

Activity 9: Garden of Jupiter

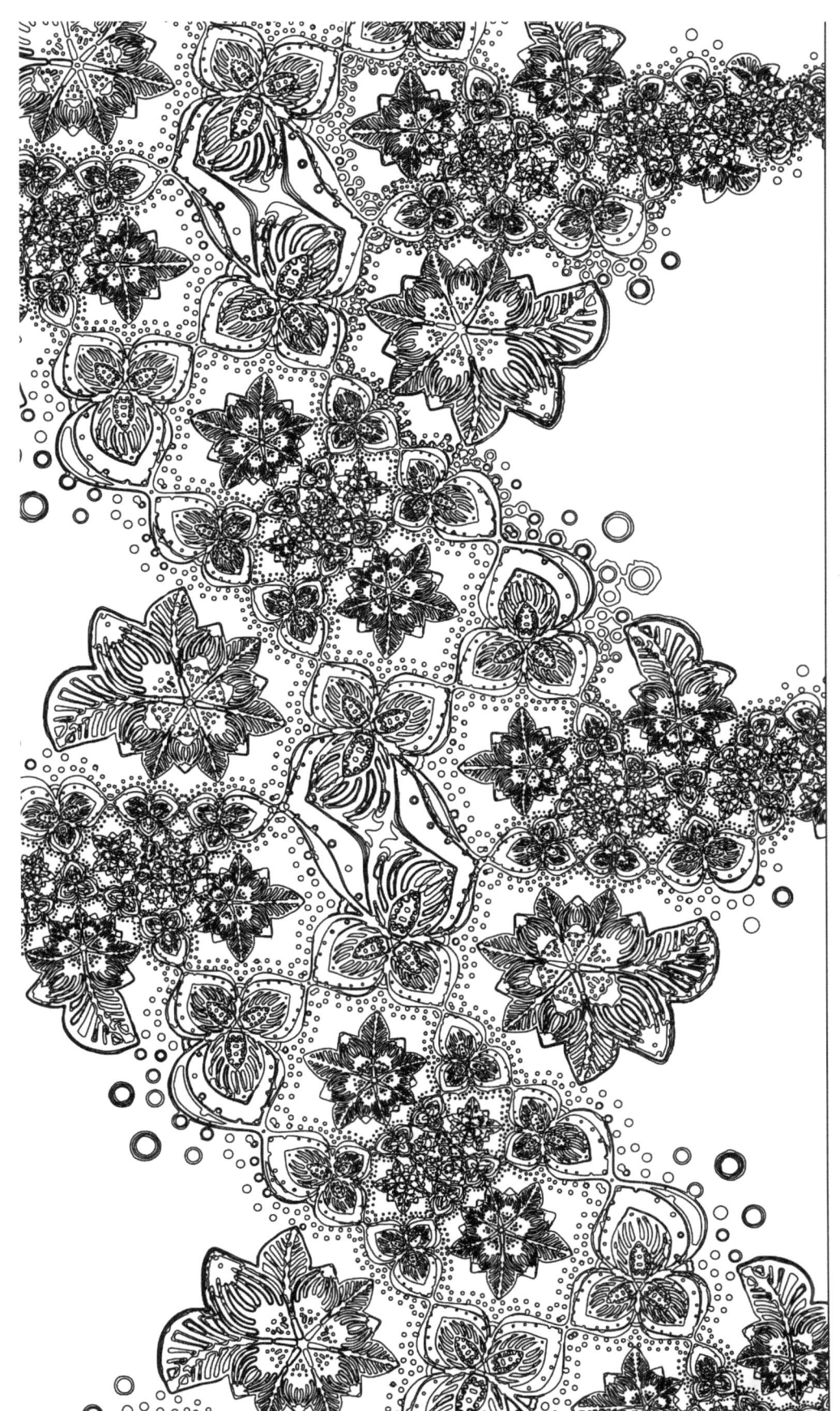

Activity 10: Haiden

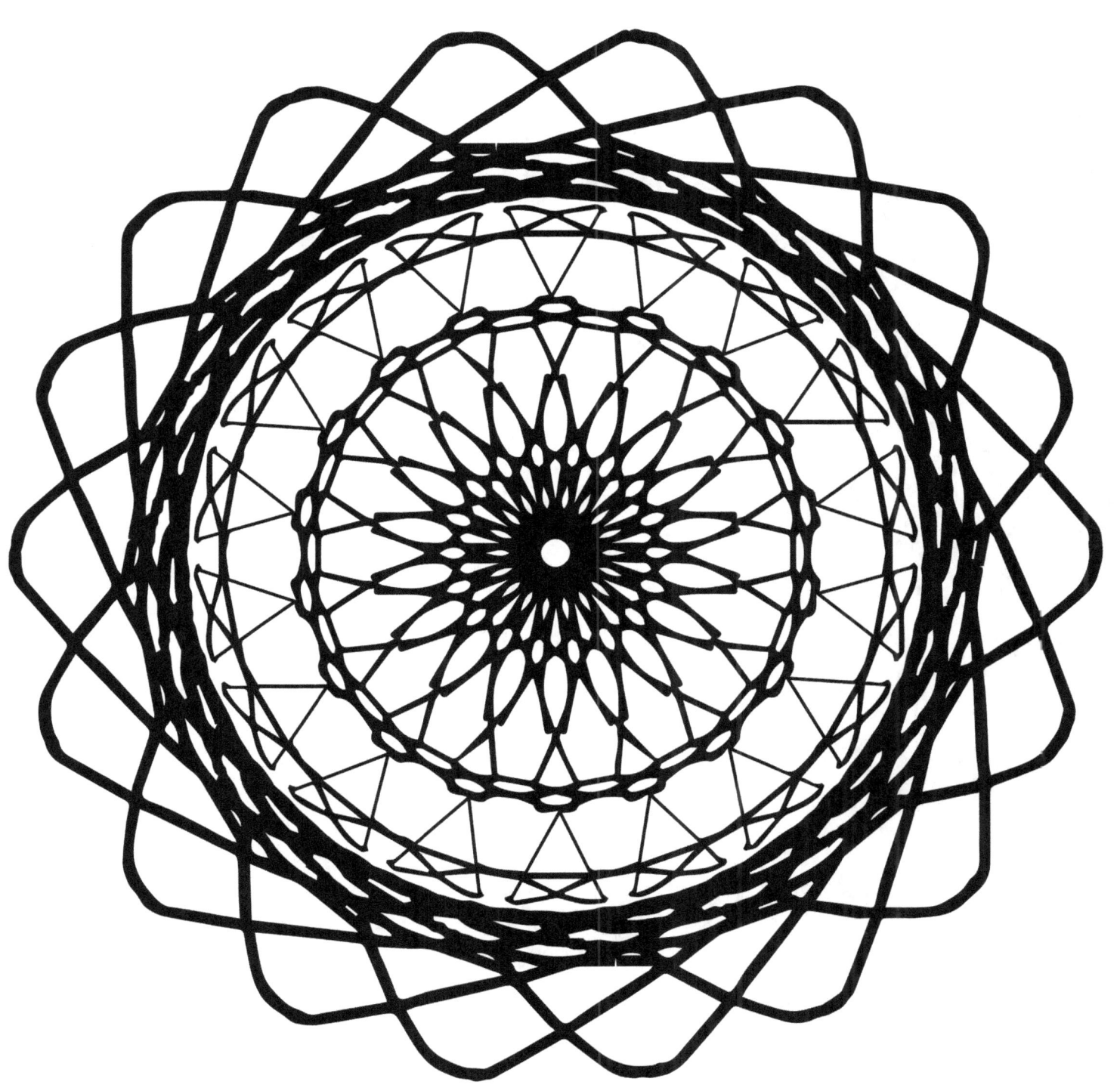

Activity 11: Gateway to Shinto

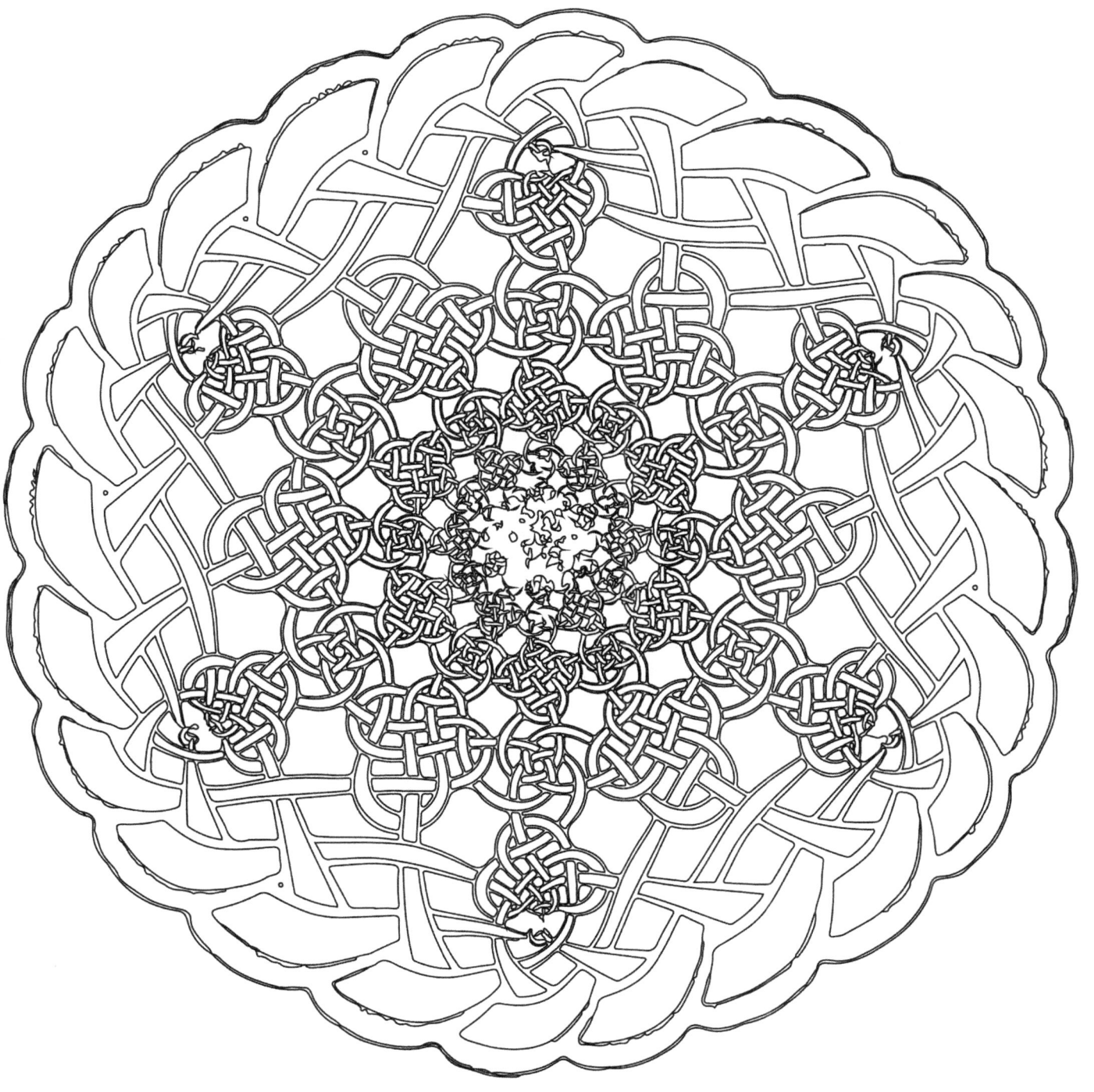

Activity 12: Secret of Taoism

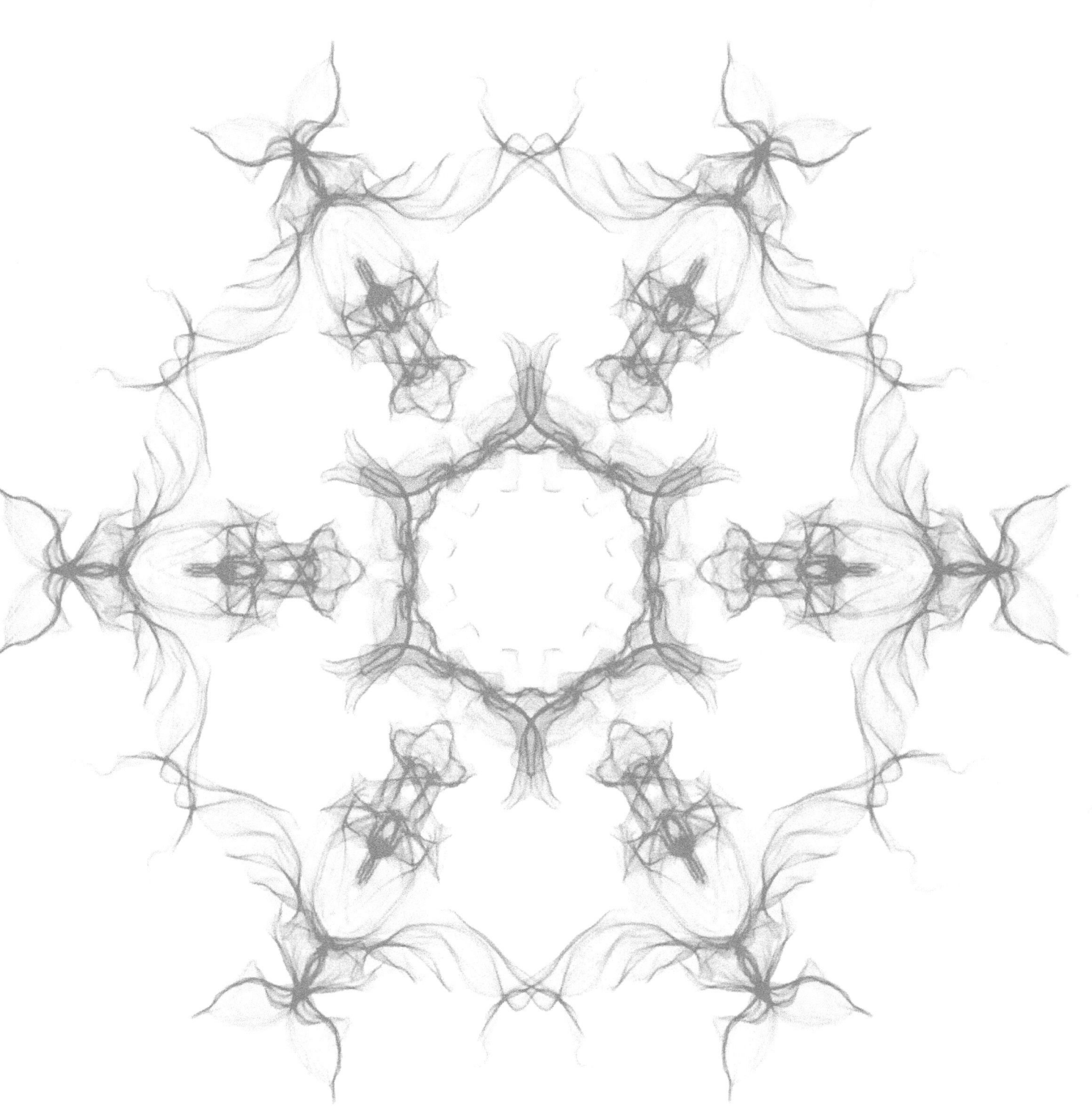

Activity 13: Zhang

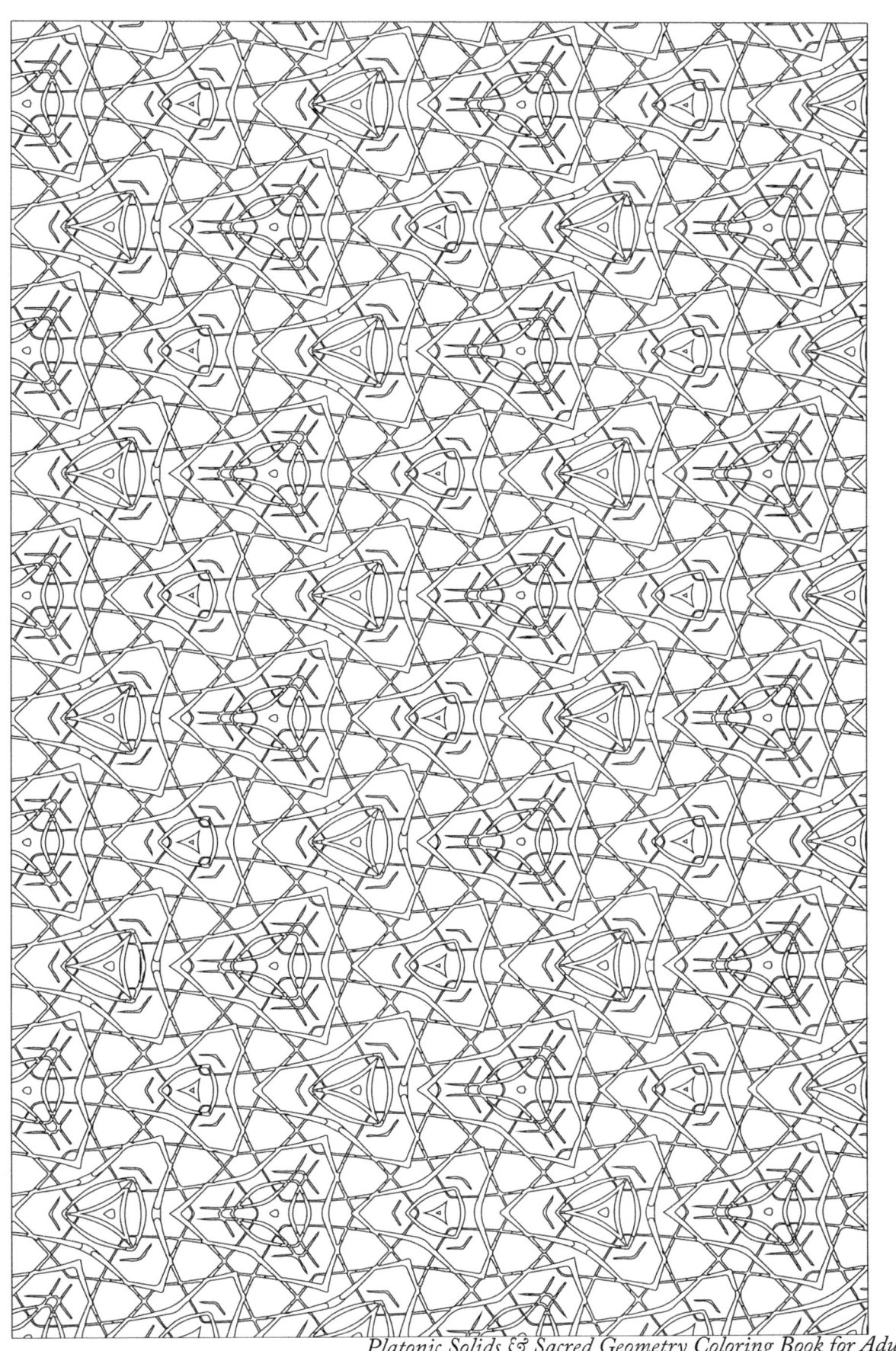

Activity 14: Seed of Life

Activity 15: Star

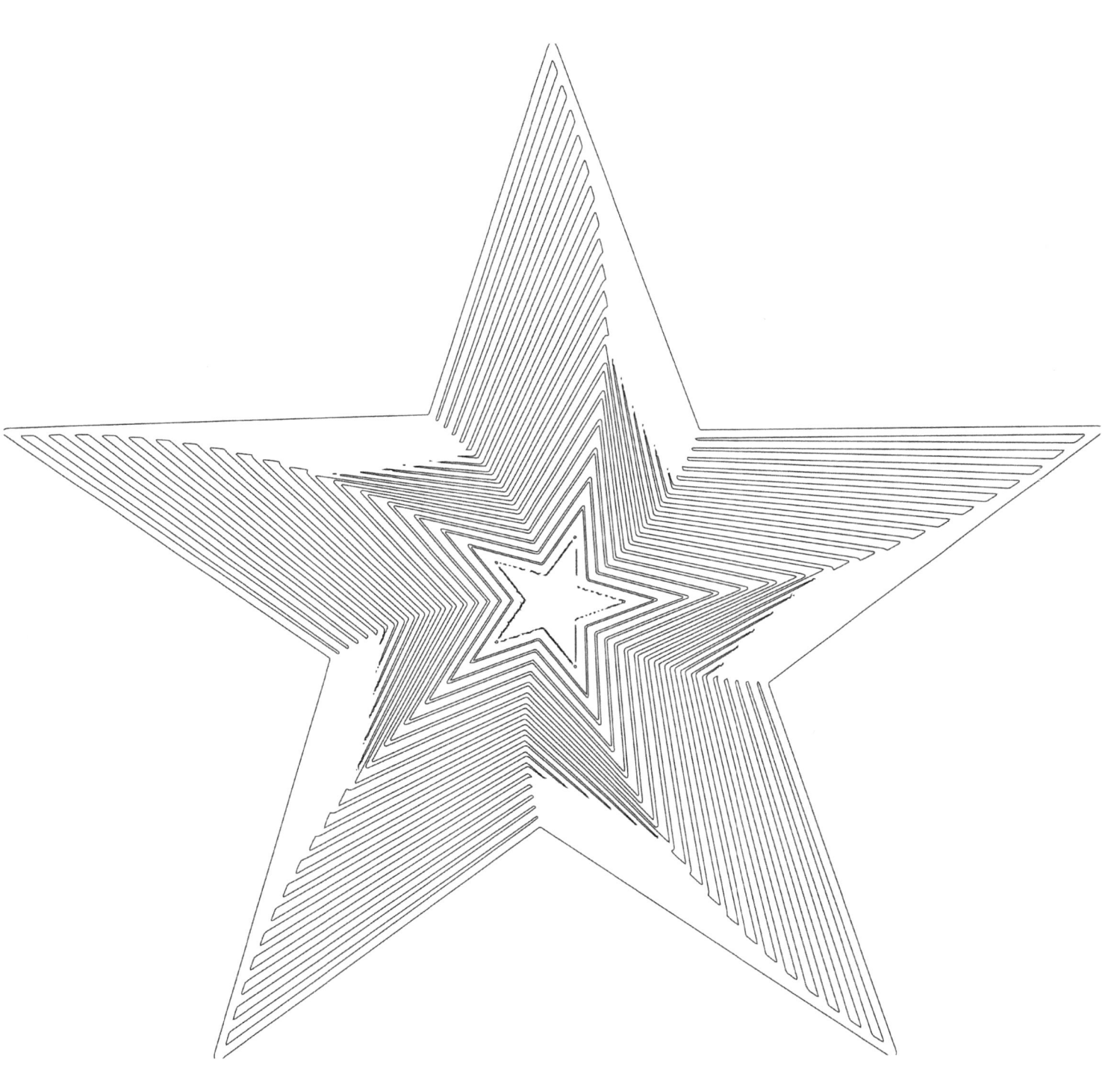

Activity 16: Triangulation Theory

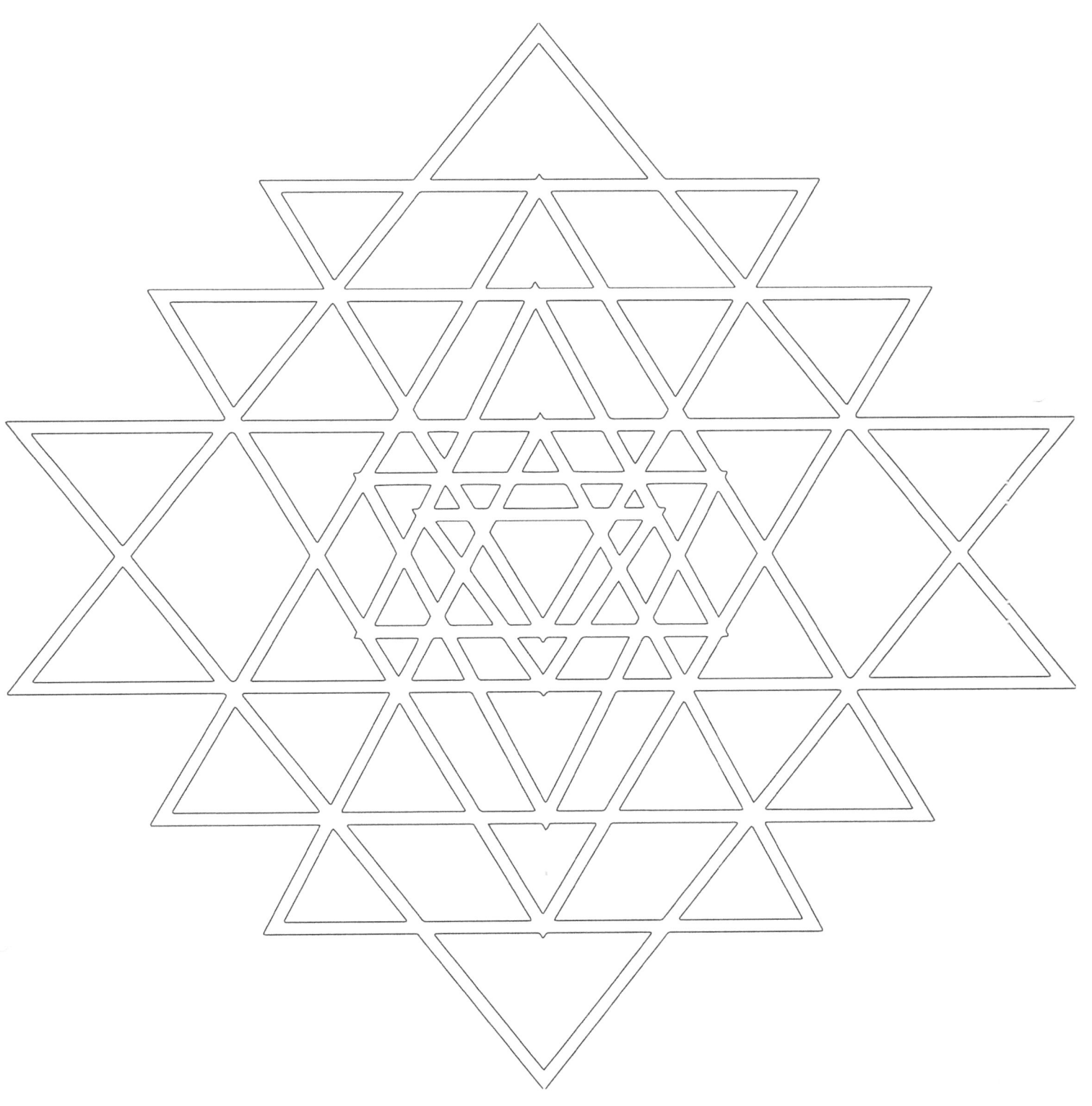

Platonic Solids & Sacred Geometry Coloring Book for Adults

Activity 17: Saint Germain

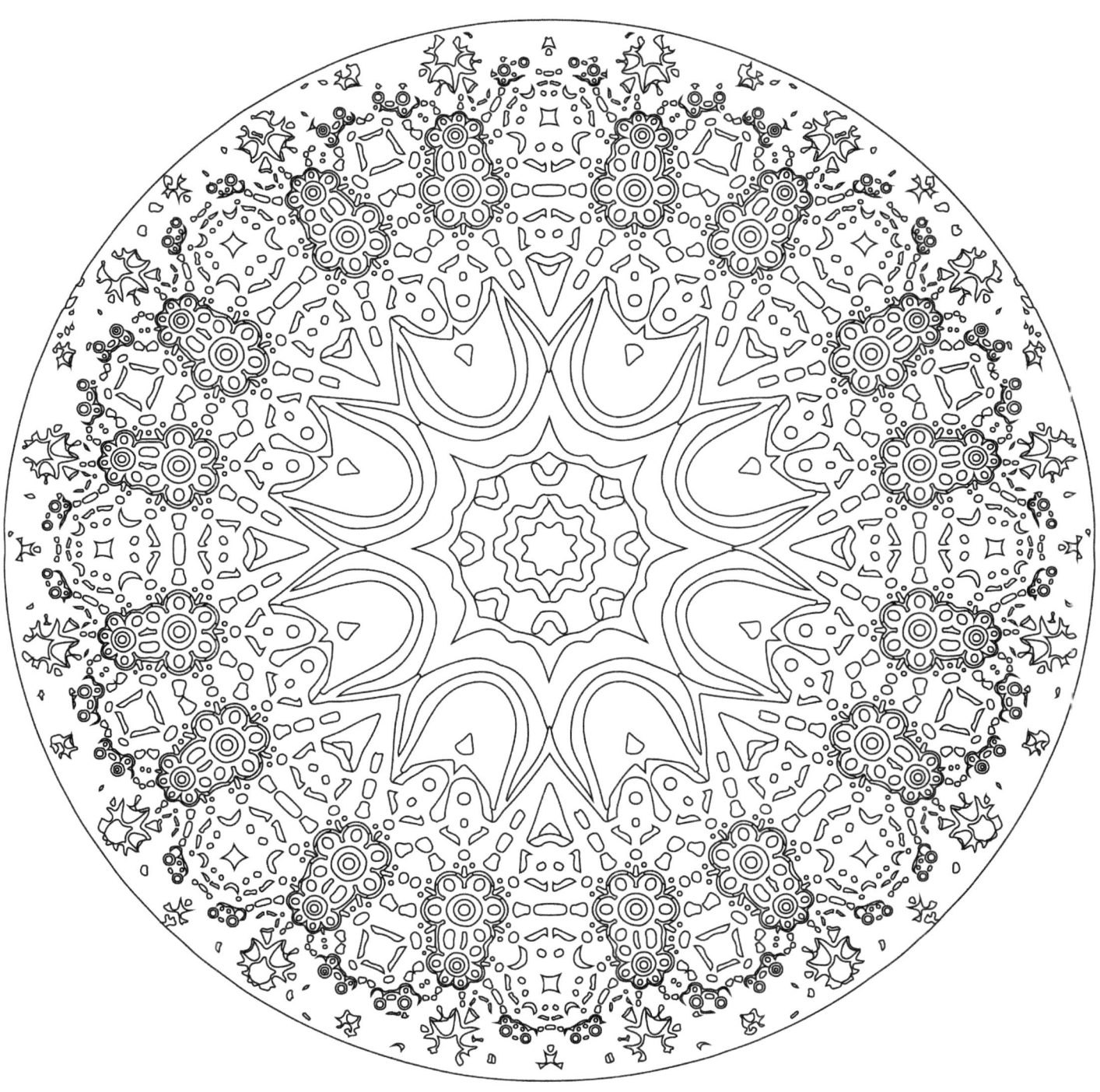

Activity 18: Secret of Nature

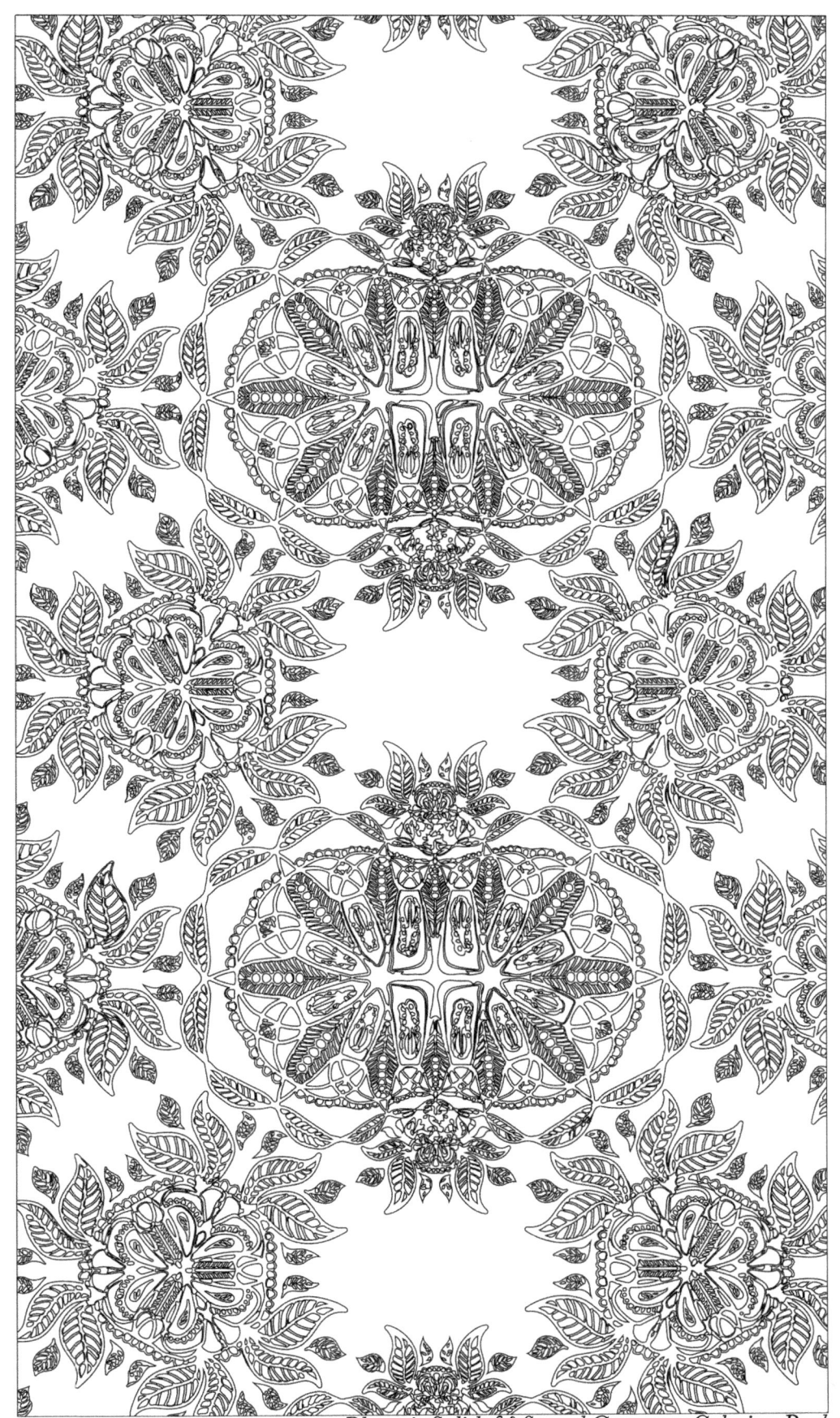

Activity 19: Vulgate Cycle

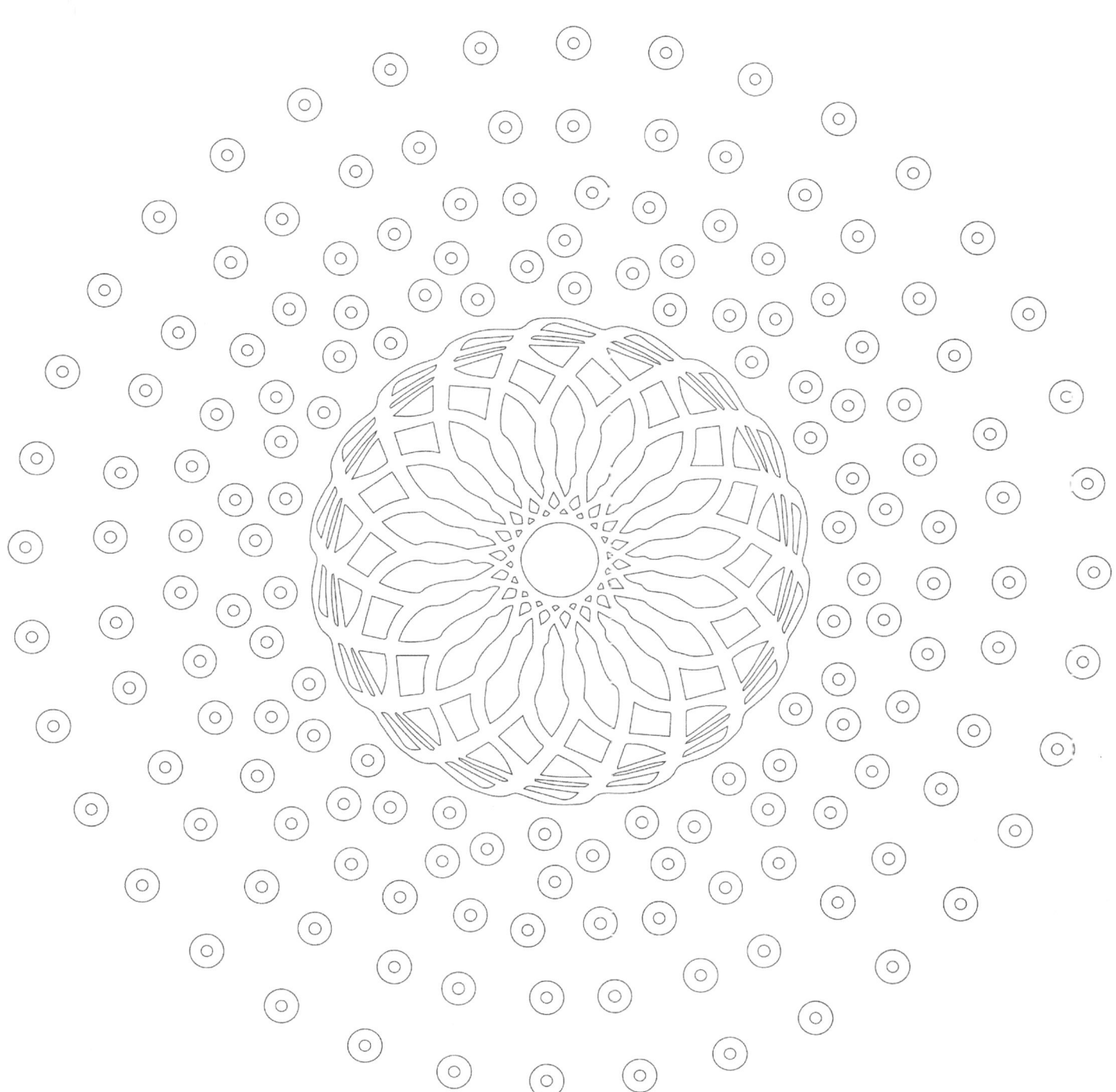

Platonic Solids & Sacred Geometry Coloring Book for Adults

Activity 20: Electricity & Magnetism

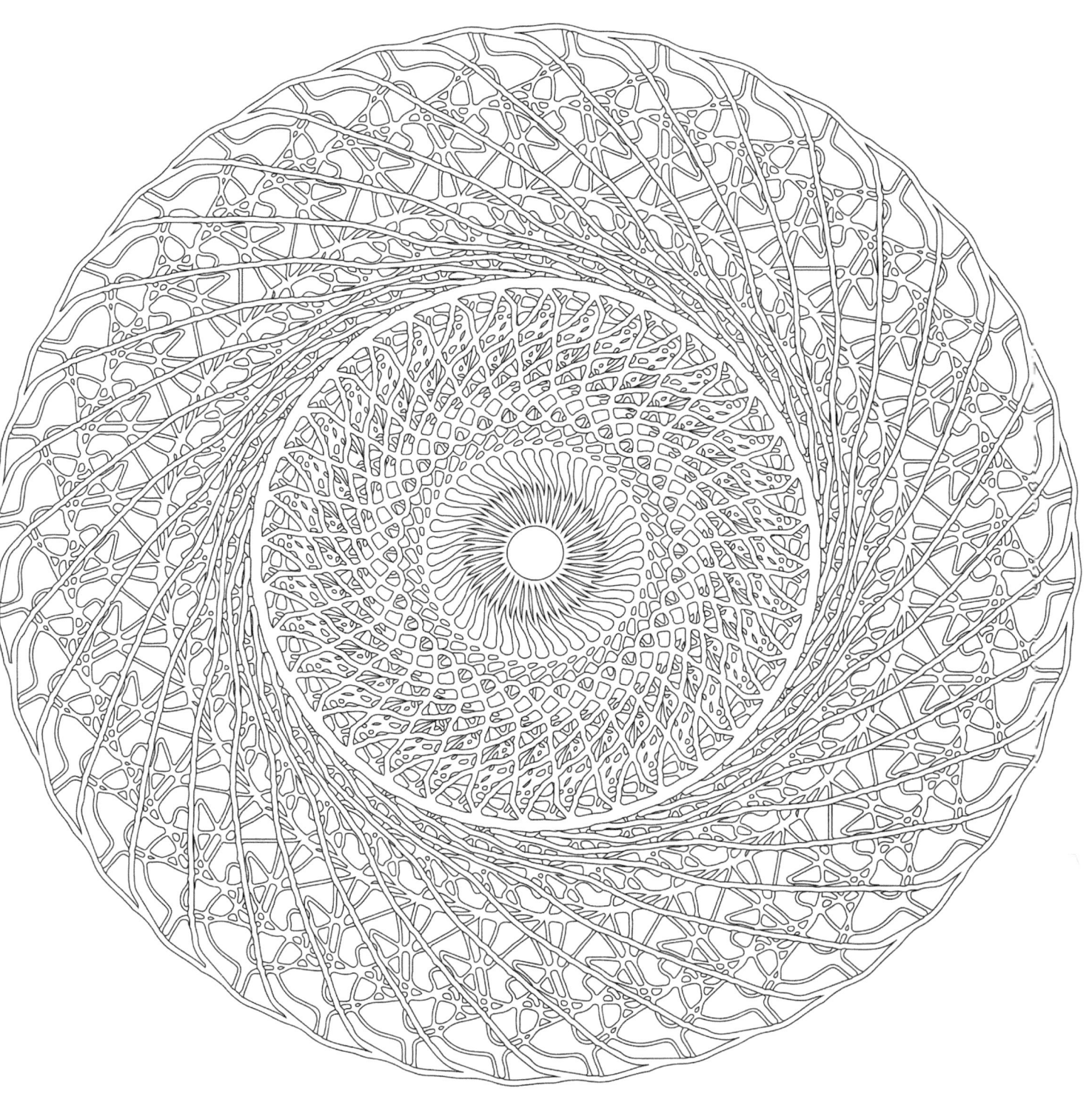

Activity 21: Dragon's Nest

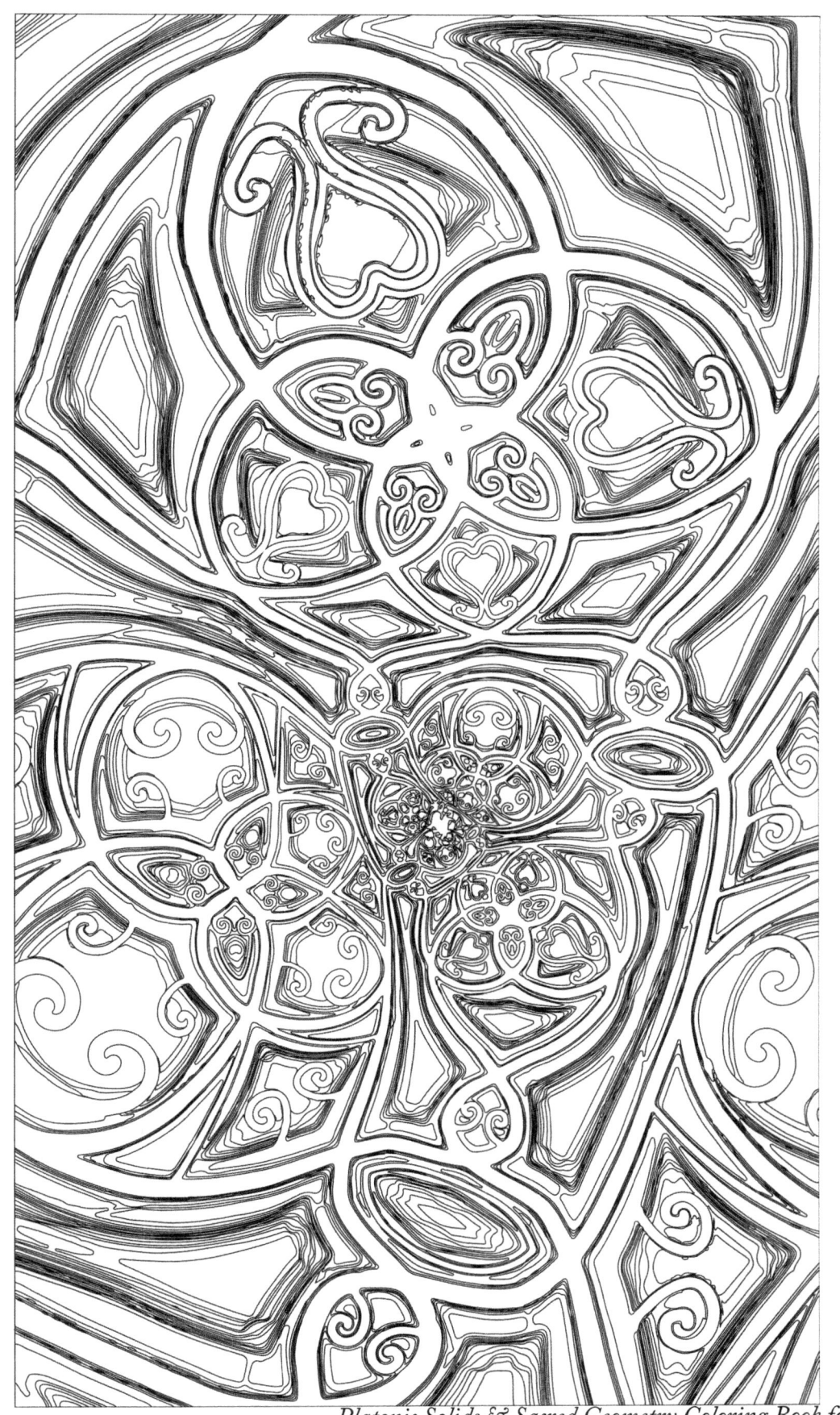

Activity 22: Perfect Symmetry

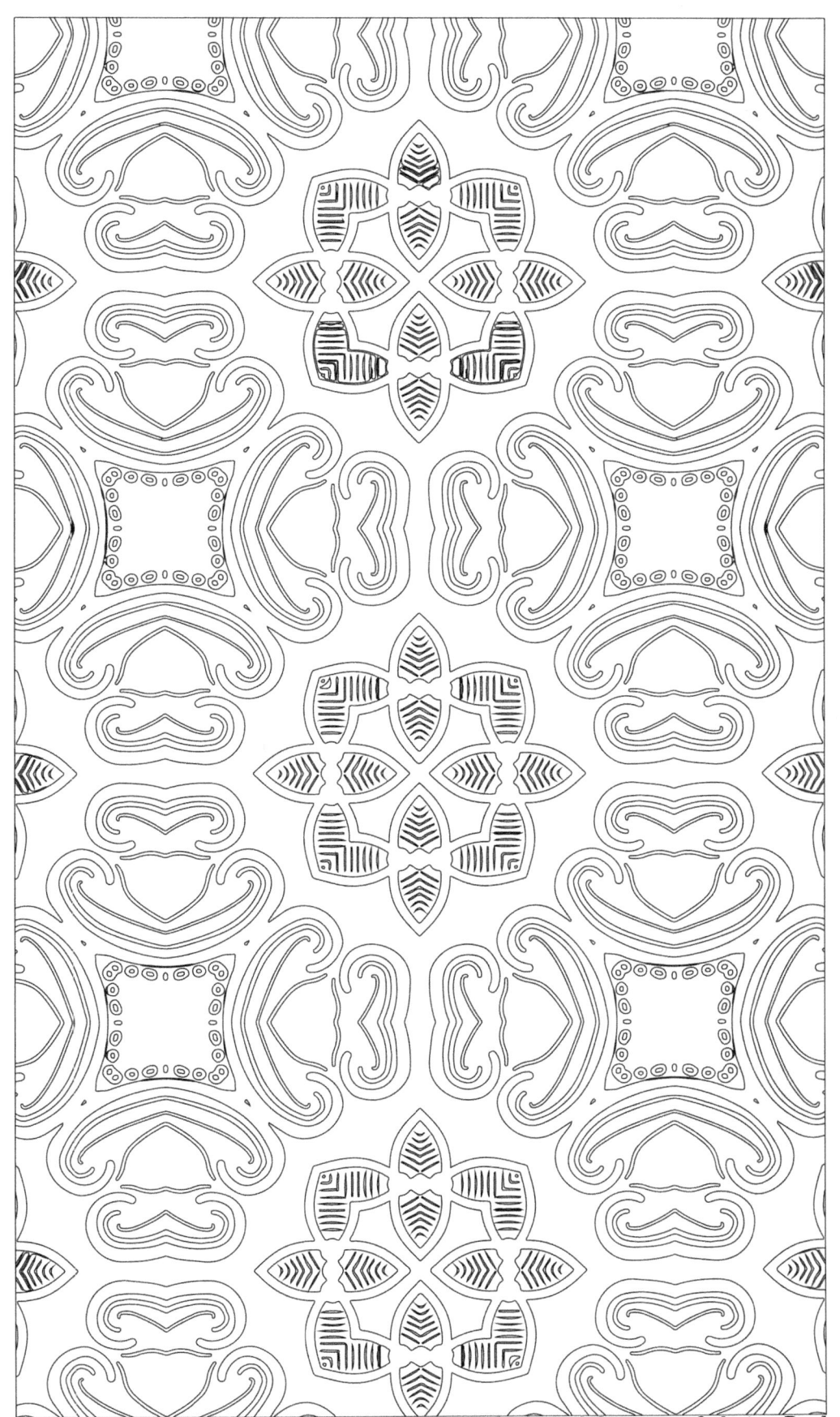

Activity 23: Autumn

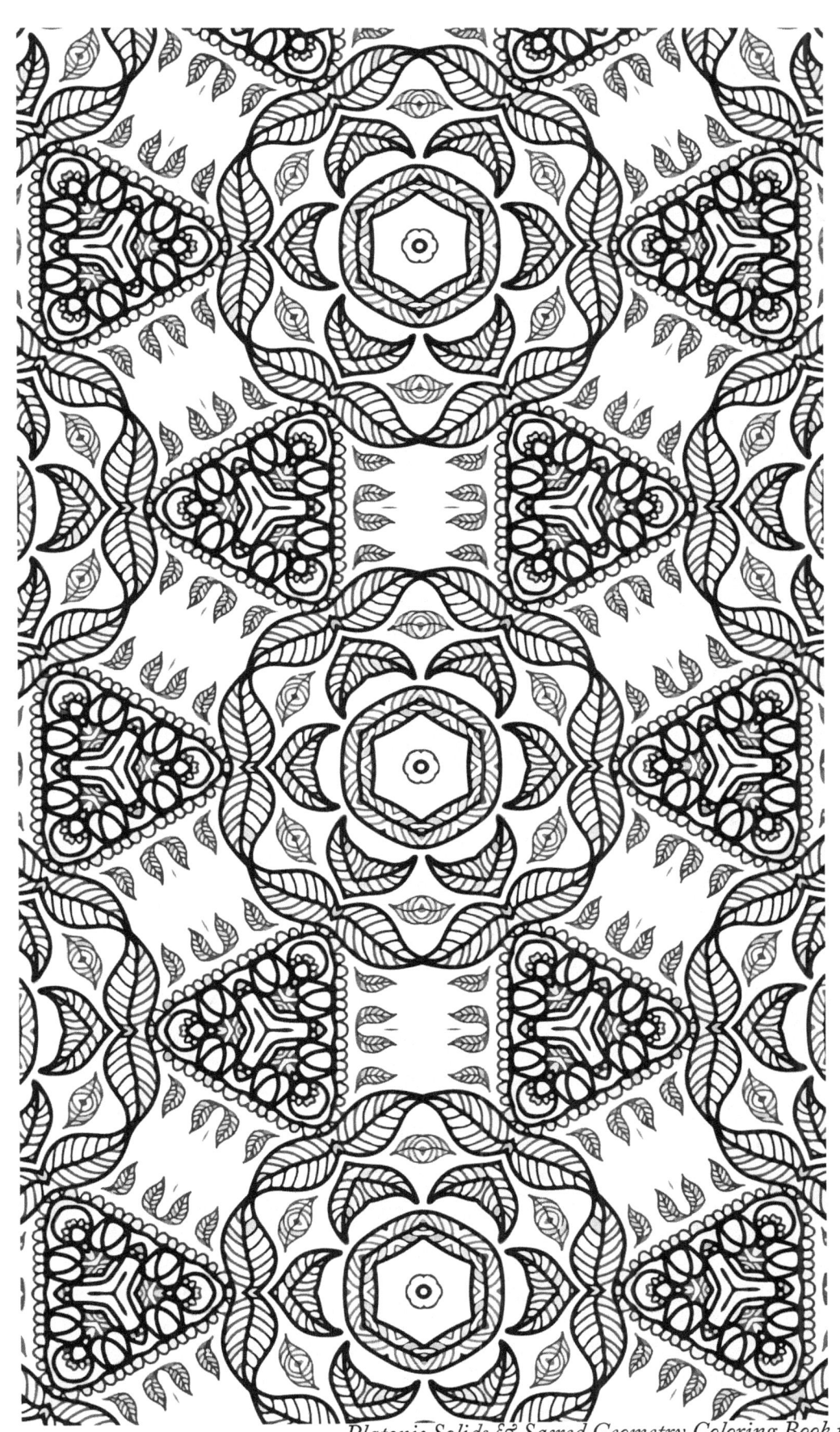

Activity 24: Network of Paths

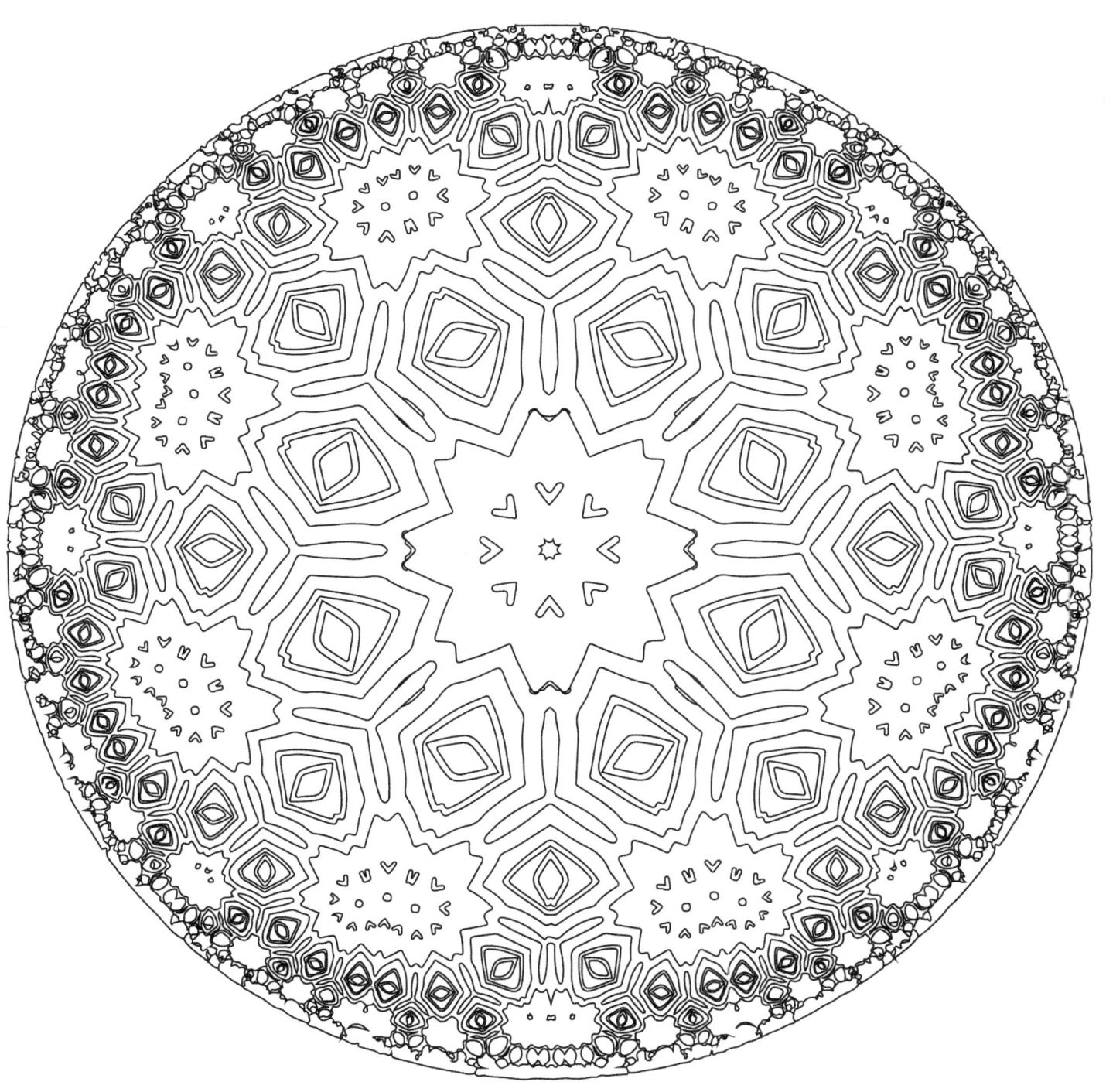

Activity 25: Renaissance

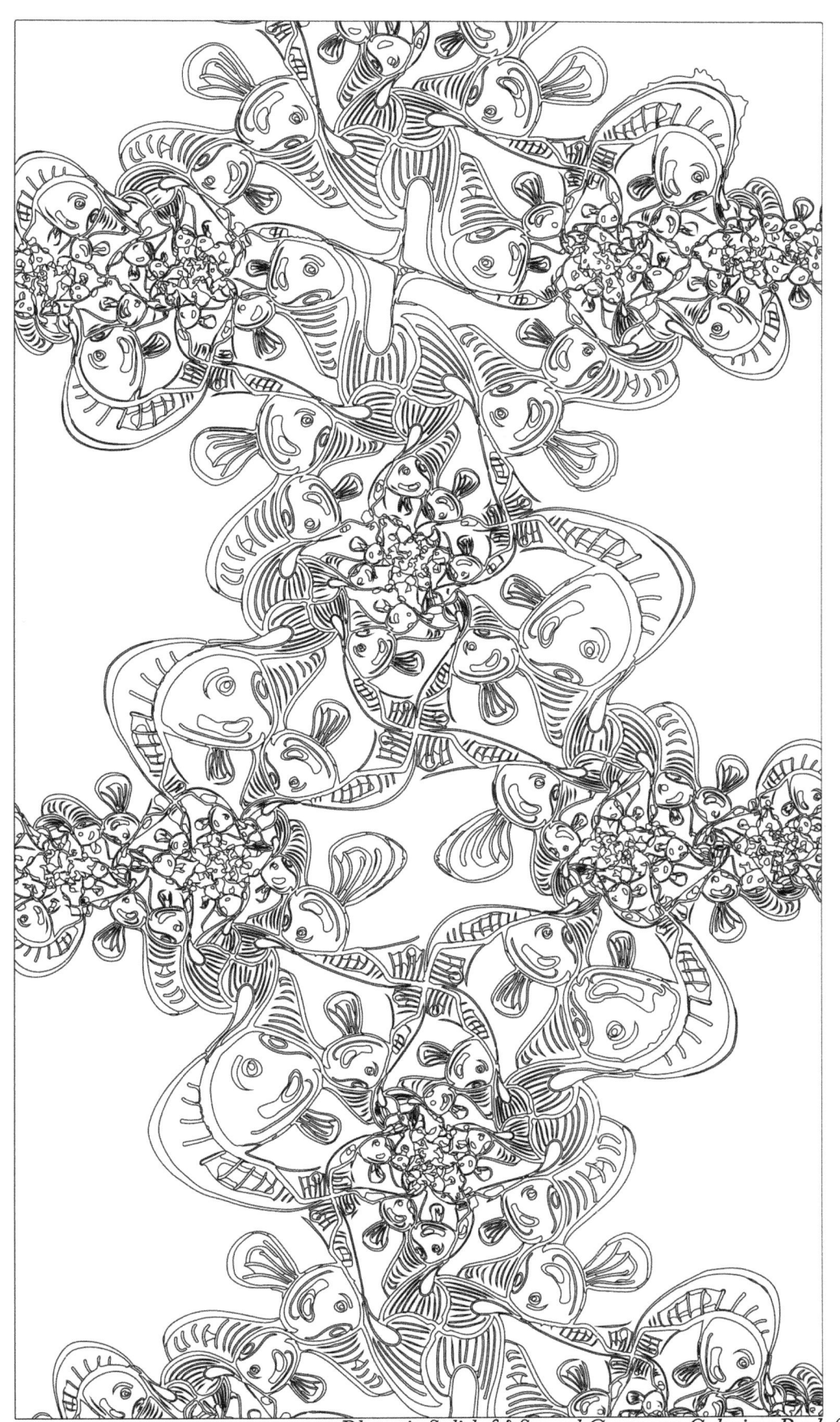

Activity 26: Twilight of the stars

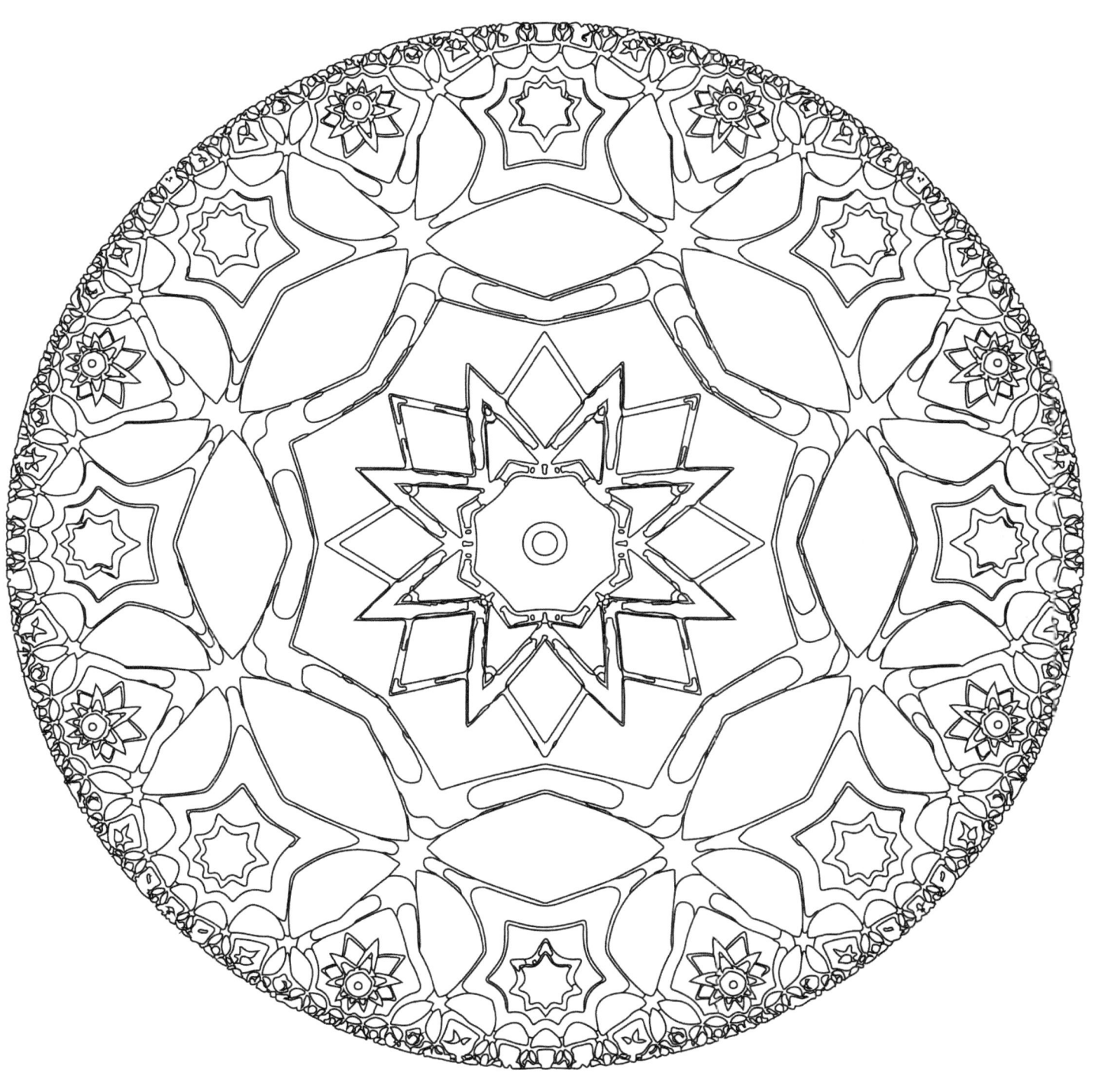

Activity 27: Wexicity

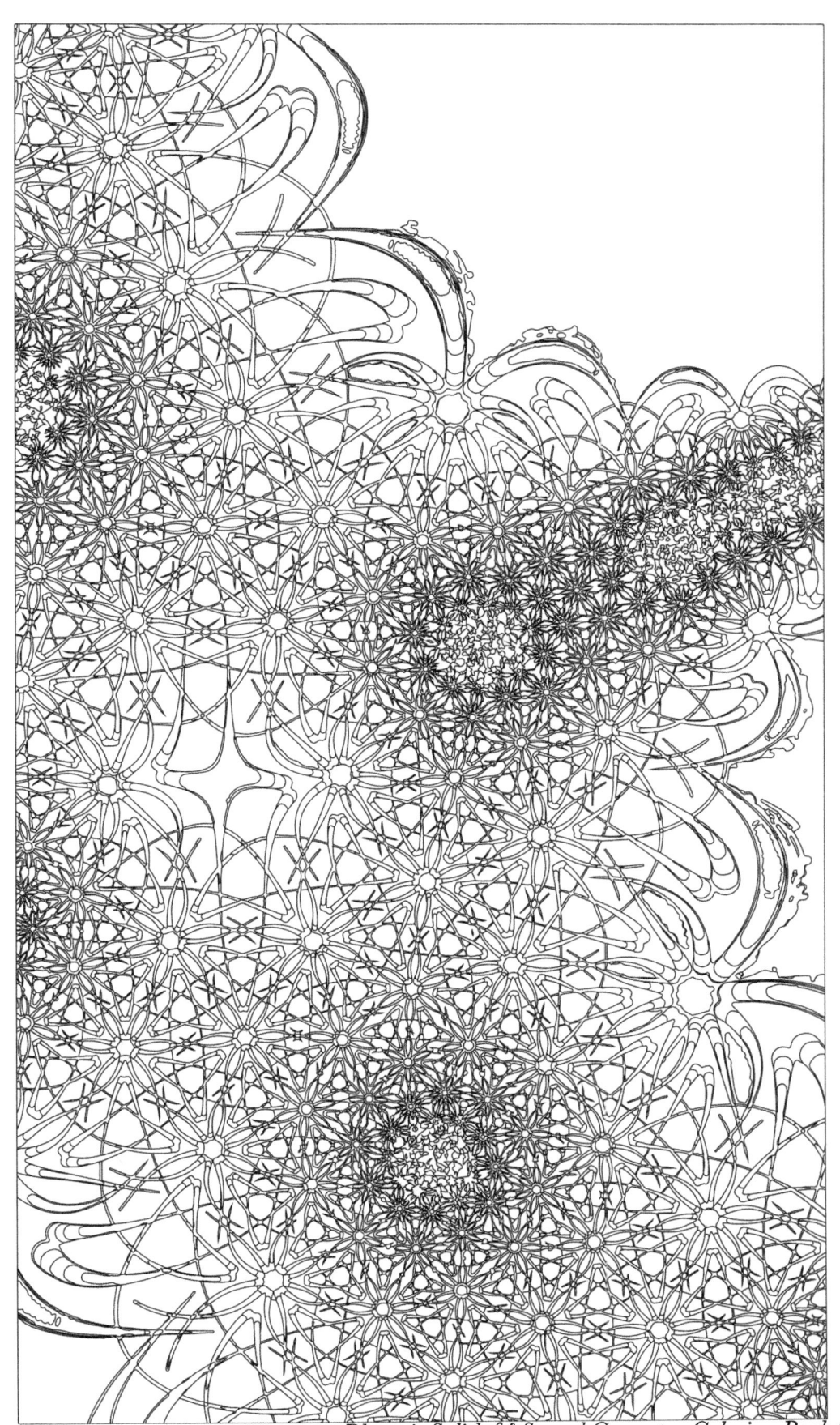

Activity 28: Mannikka

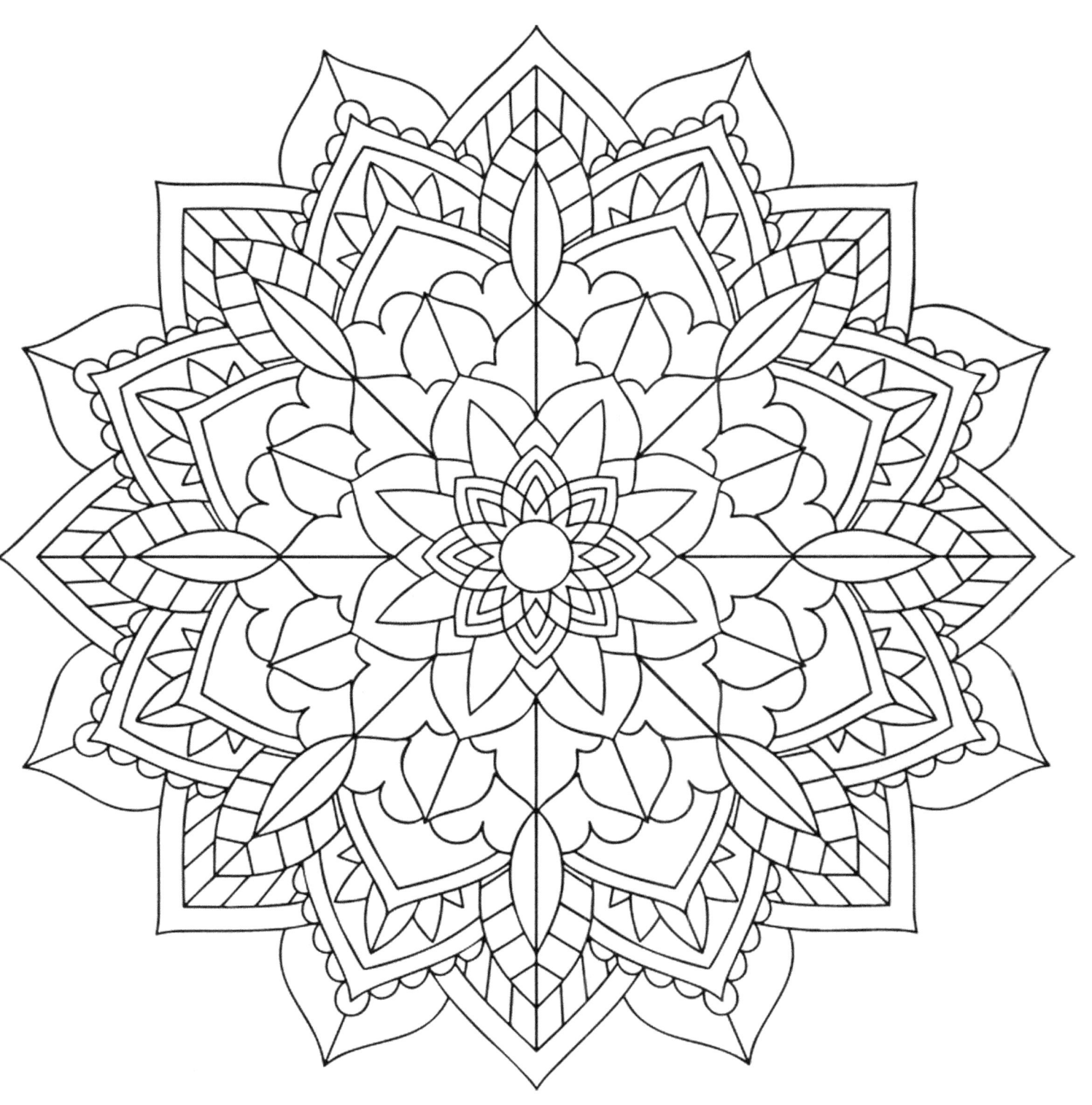

Activity 29: Derivatives of x^2

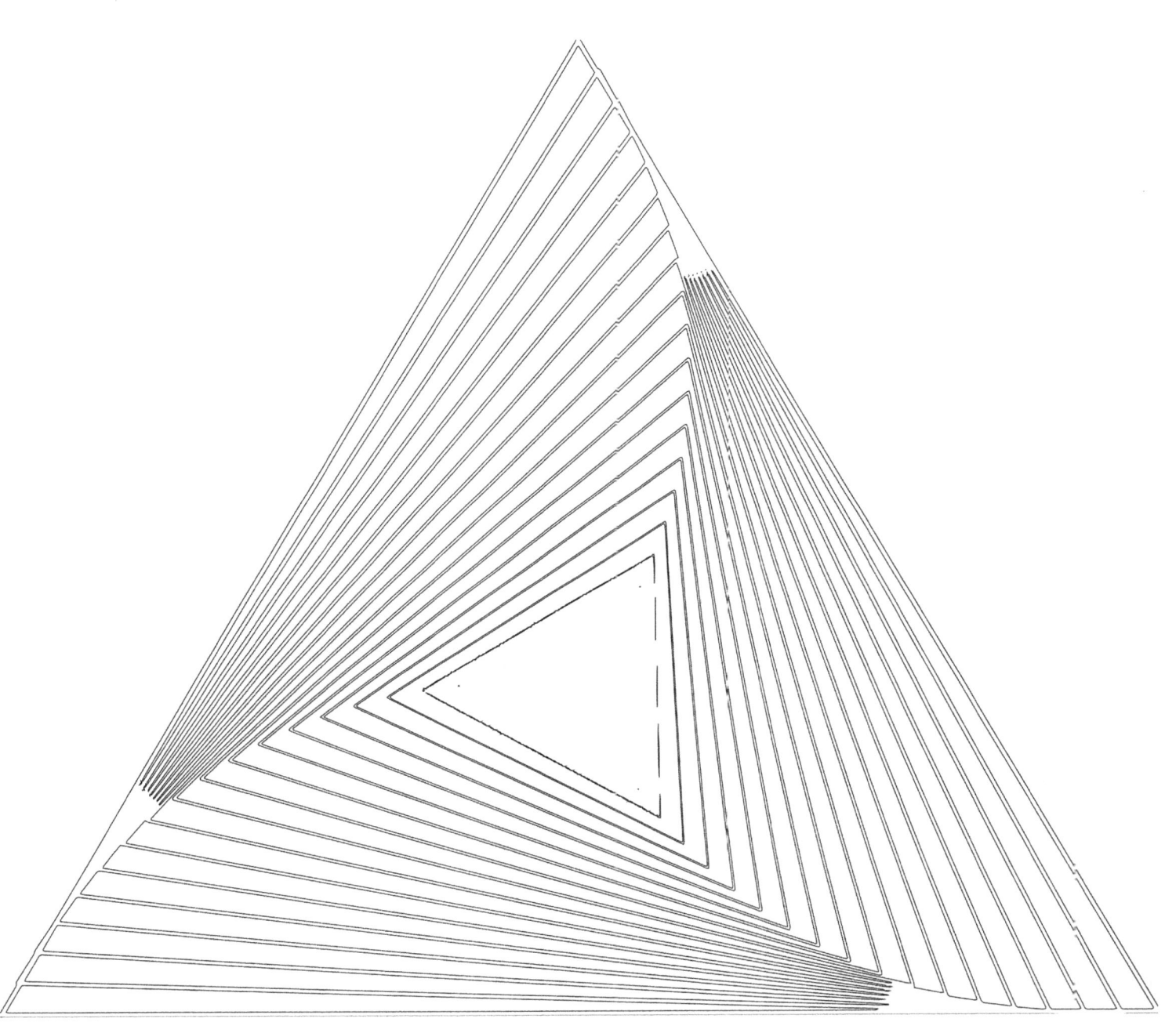

Activity 30: Devereux

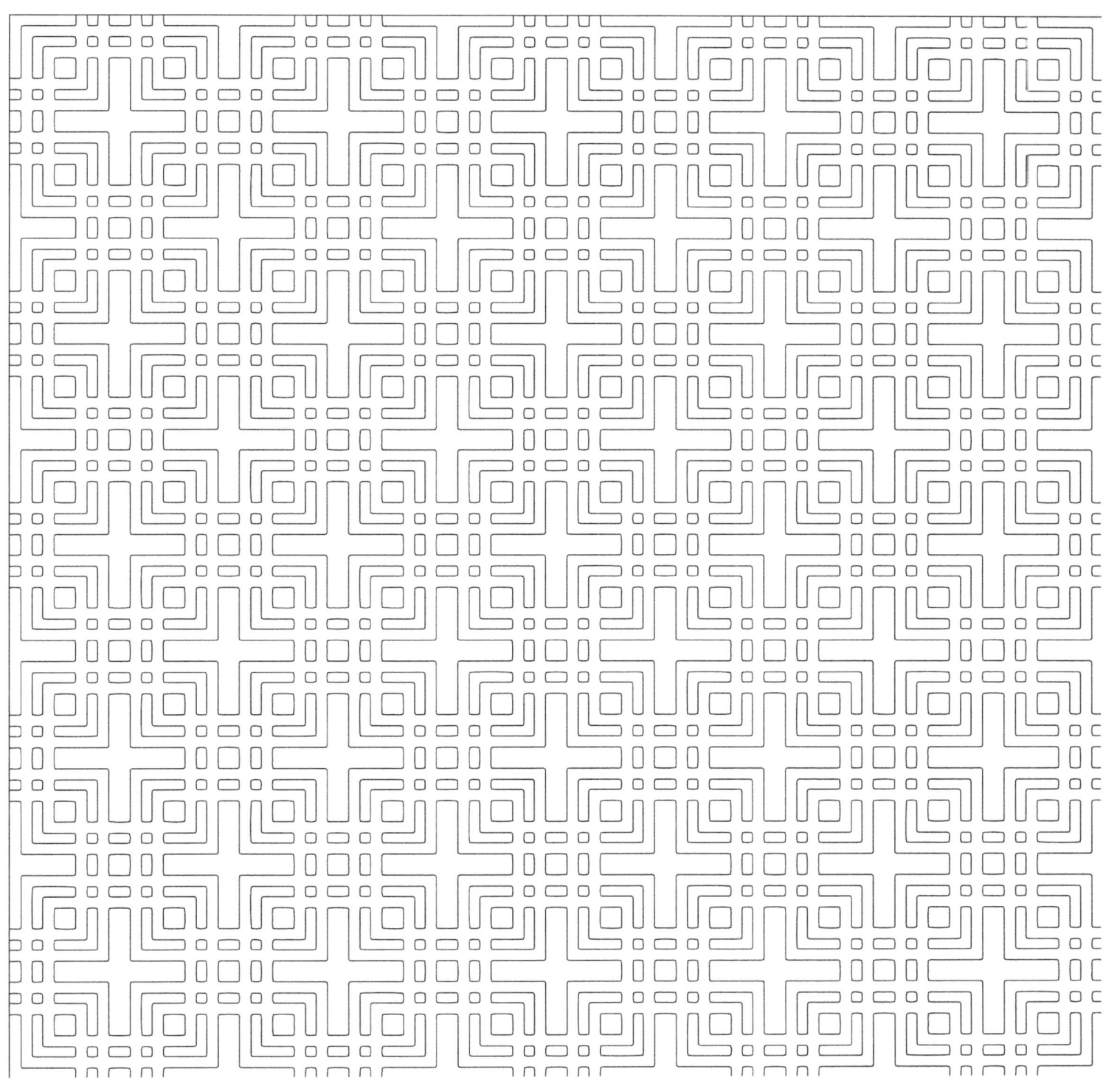

Activity 31: Chains

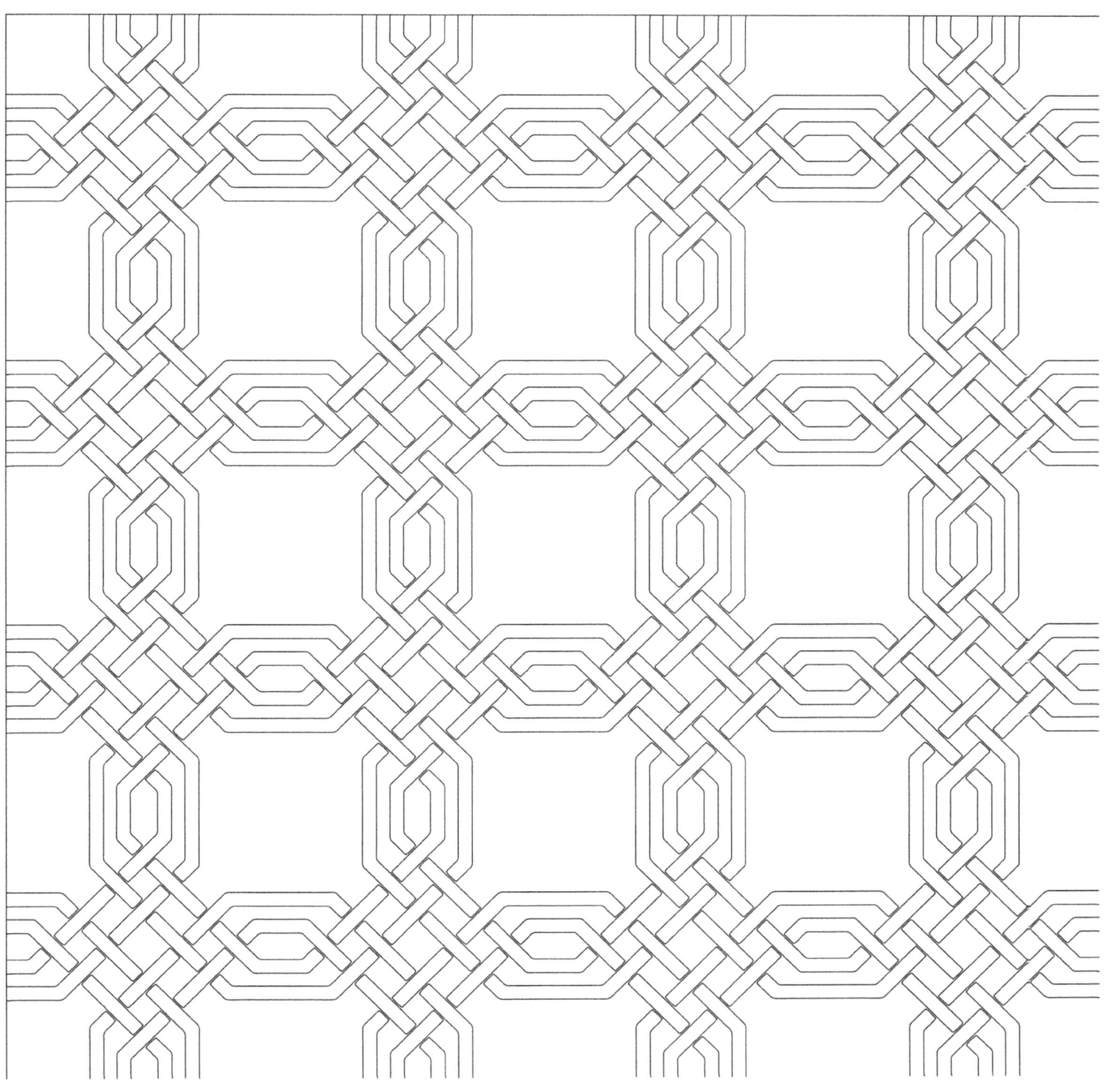

Activity 32: Glastonbury Secret

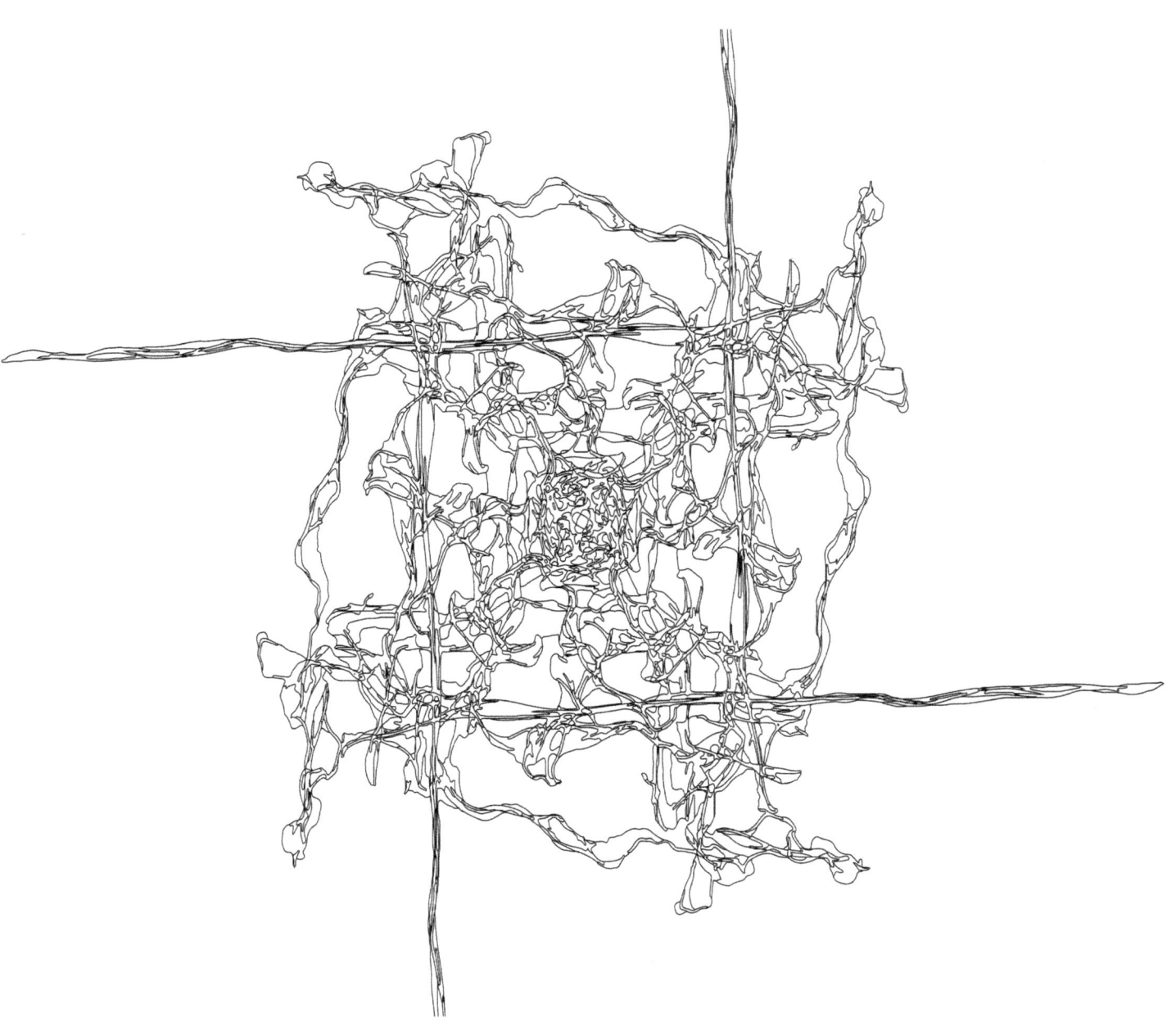

Activity 33: Eye of Providence

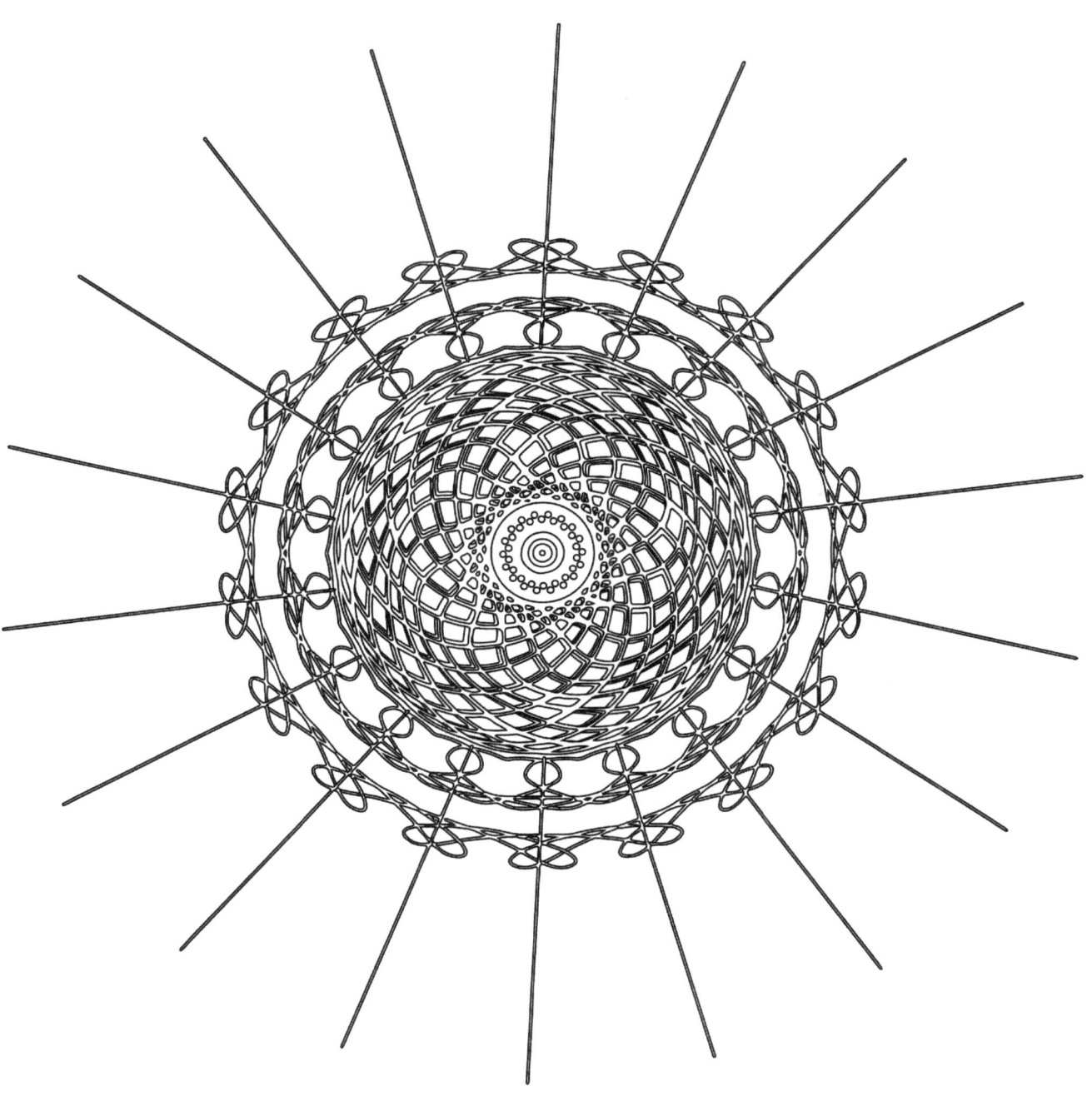

Activity 34: Godfrey de Bouillon

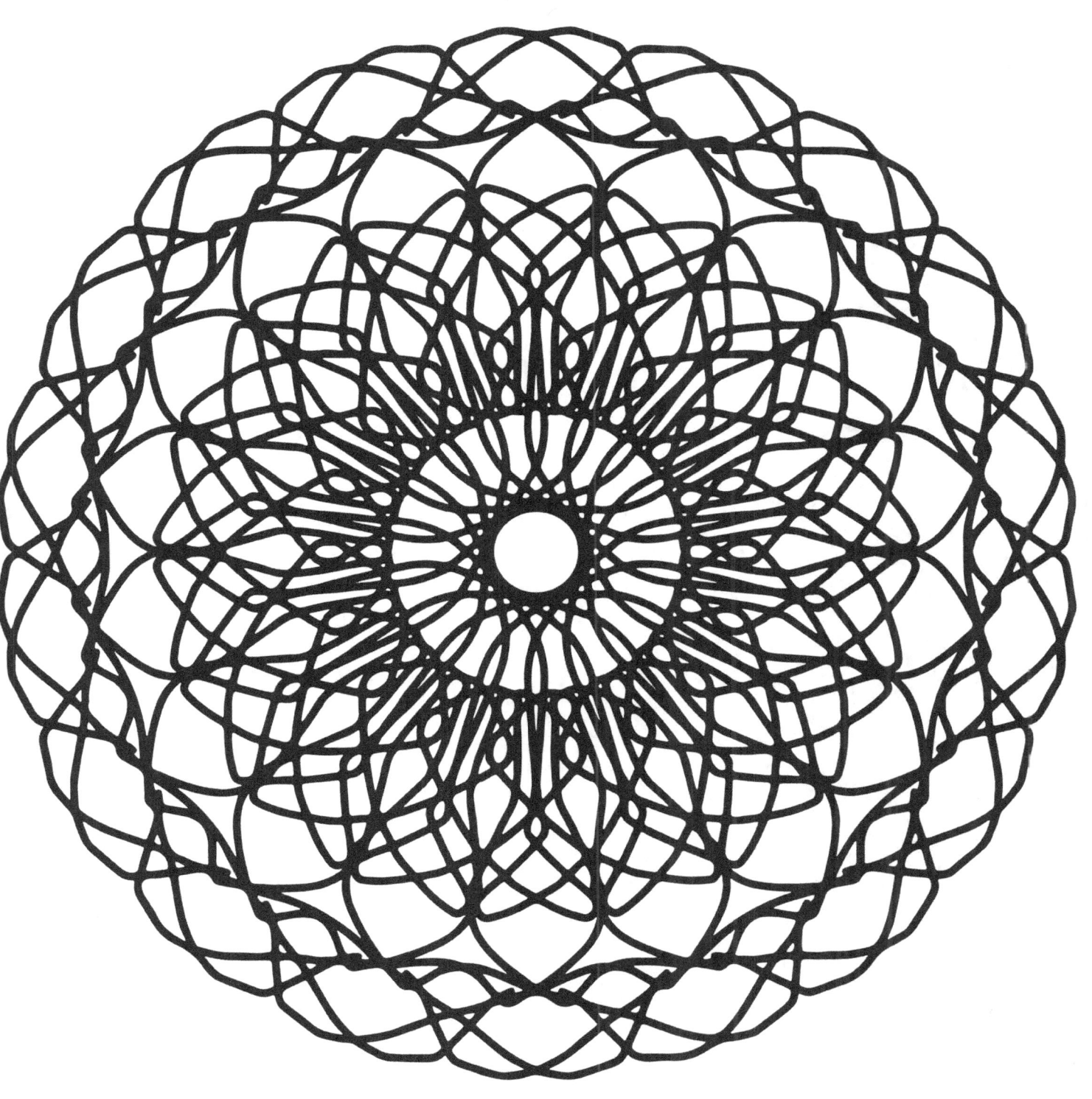

Activity 35: Shingon

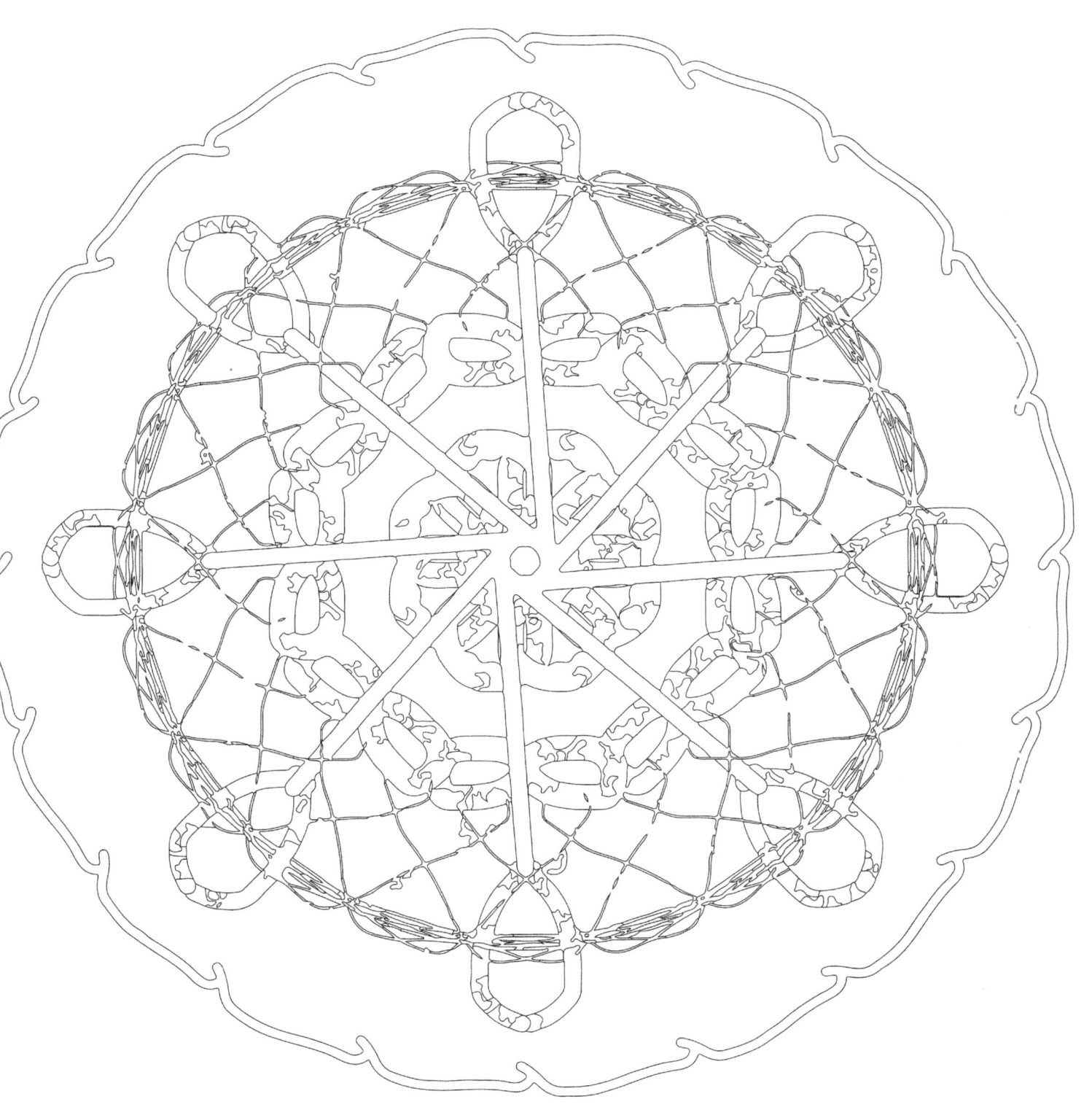

Activity 36: Point of Symmetry

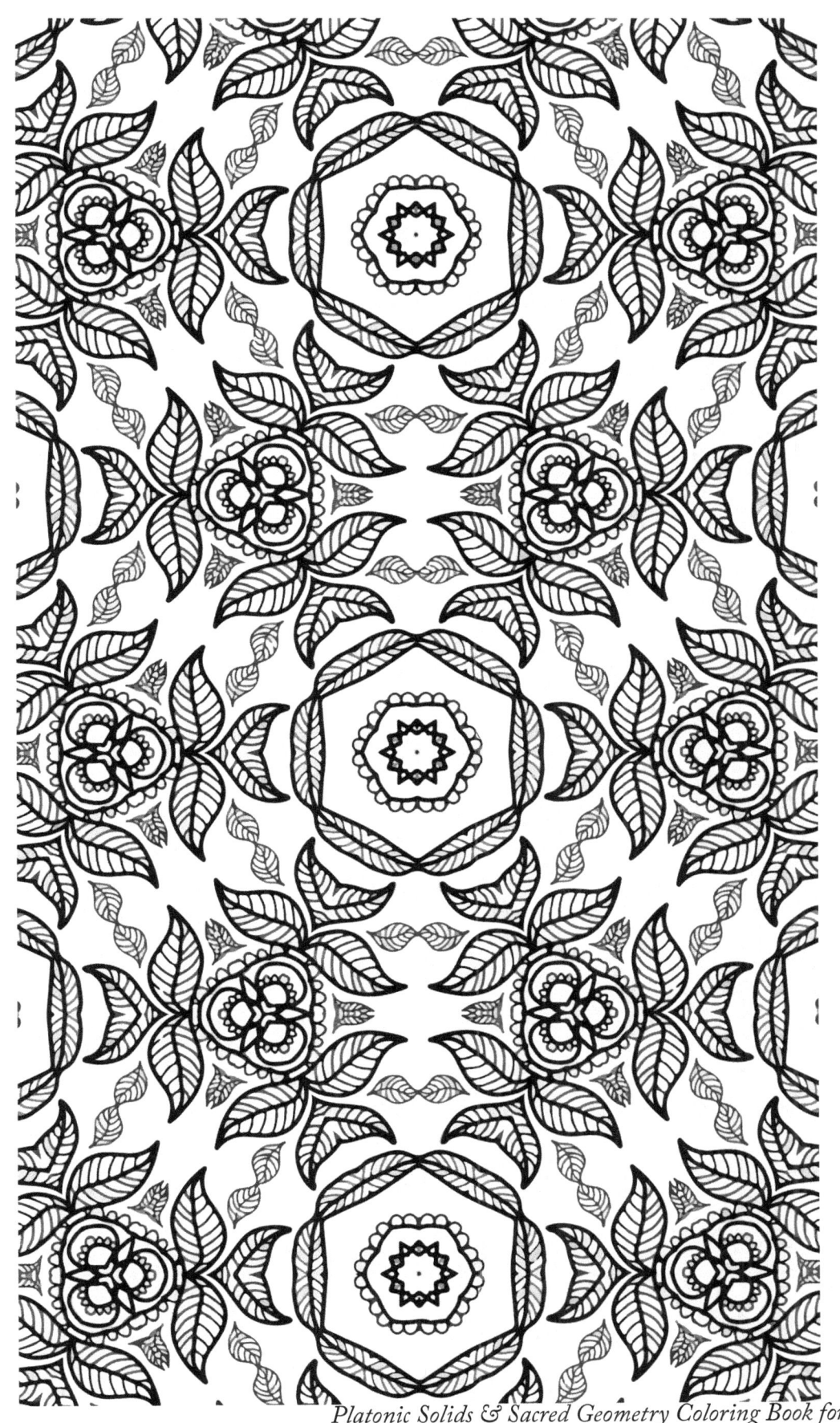

Activity 37: Peristyle Garden

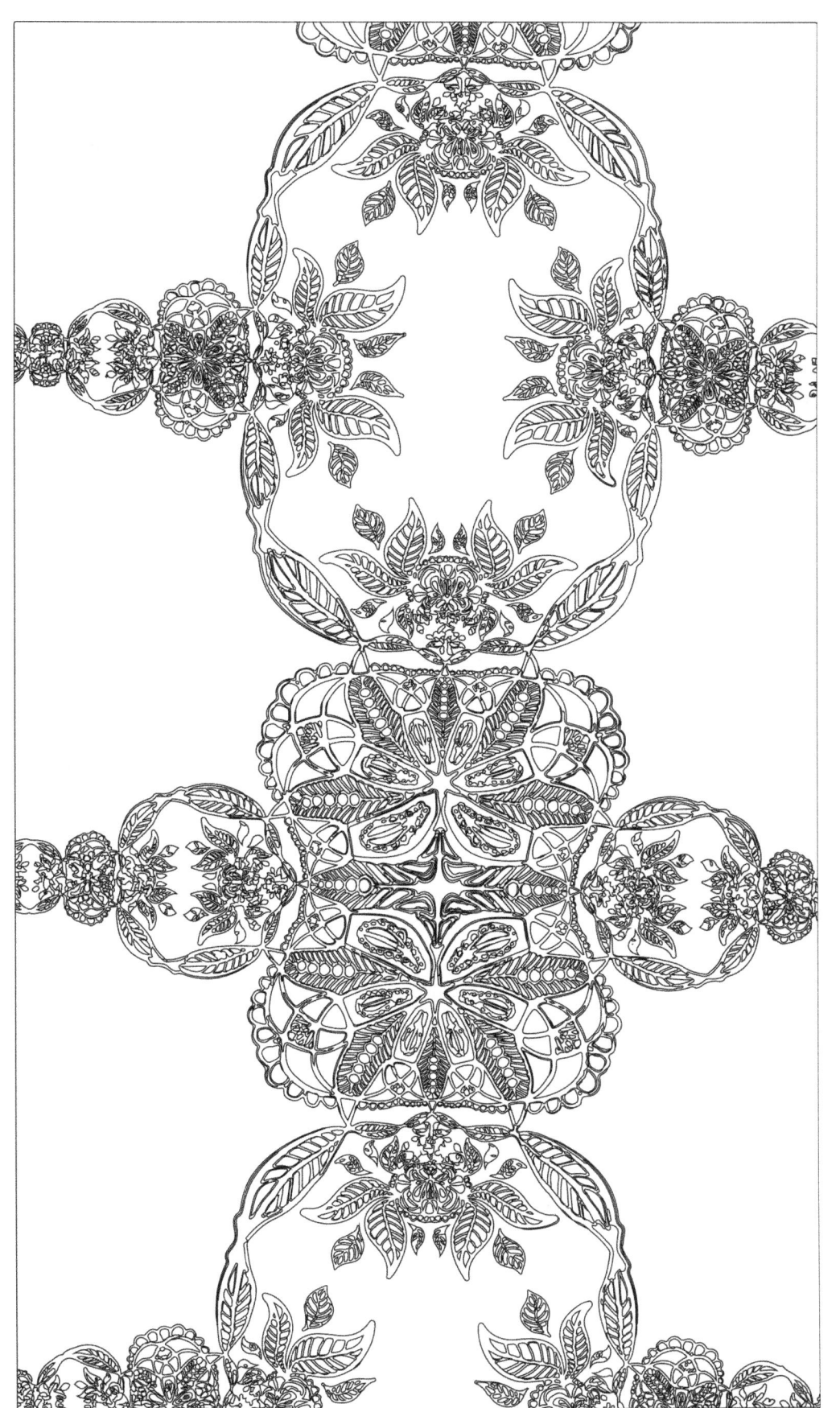

Activity 38: Curatola's last painting

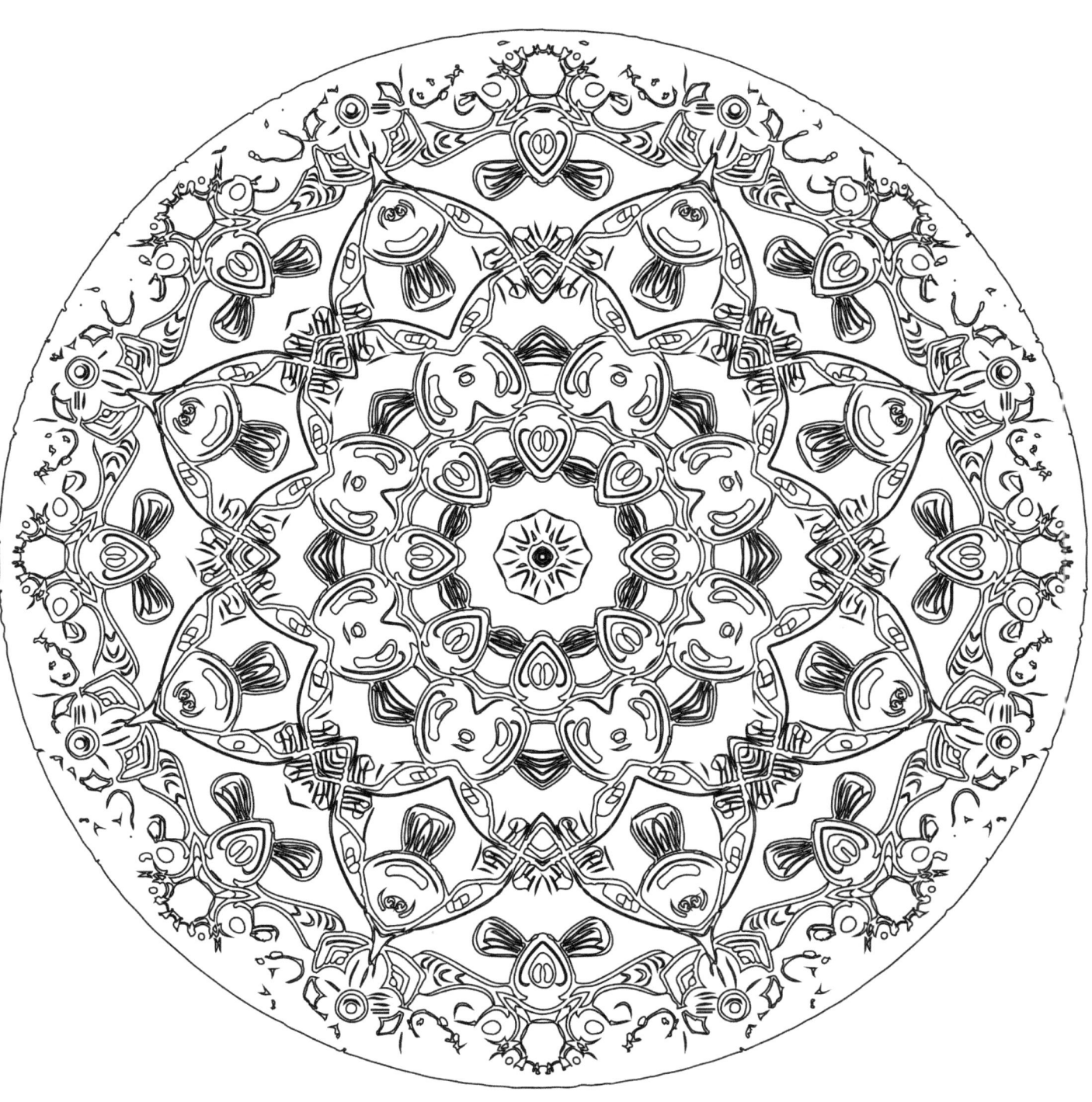

Activity 39: Circle of Love

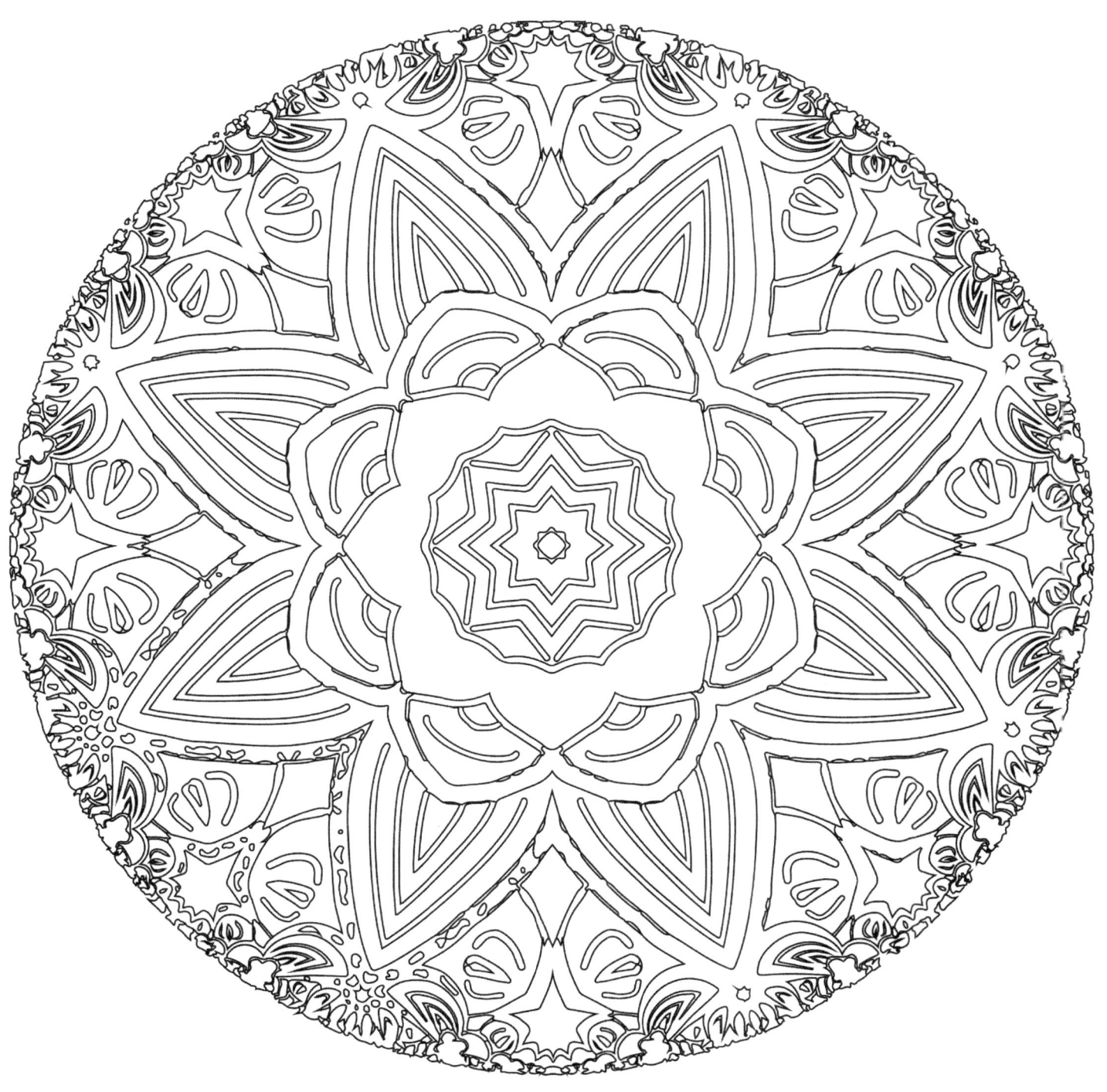

Activity 40: Mouse trap

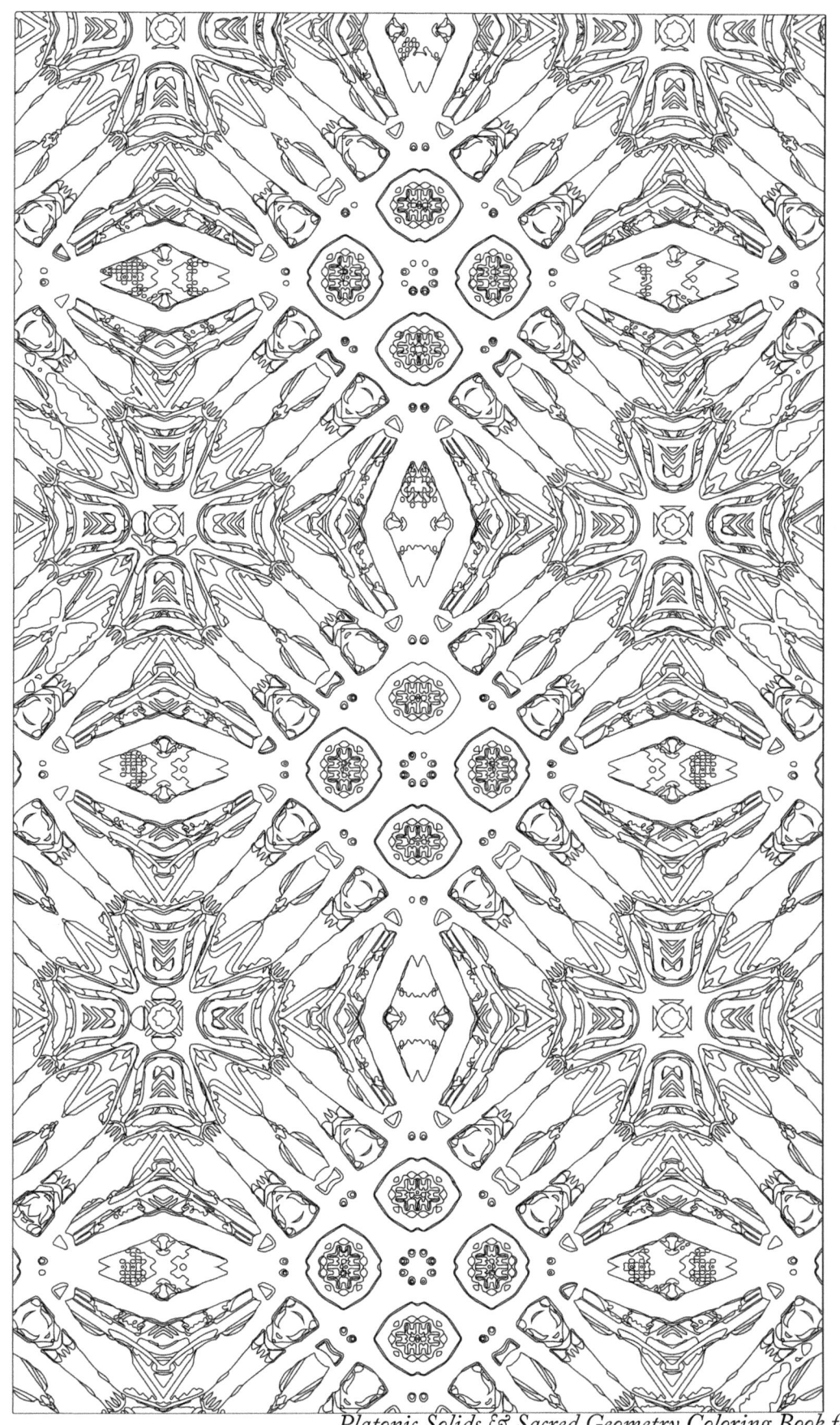

Activity 41: Hydrogen Molecule

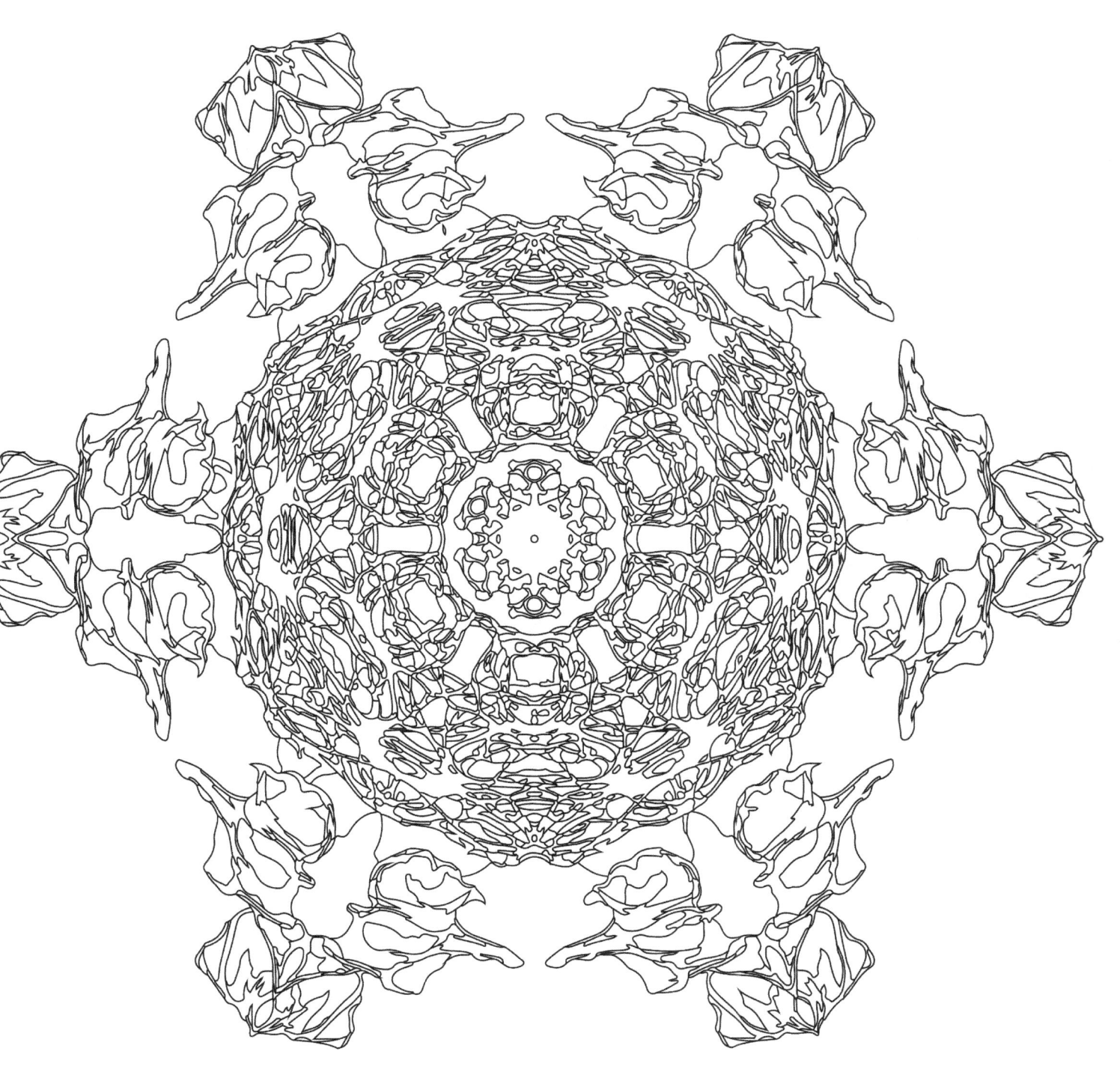

Activity 42: Infinity + 1

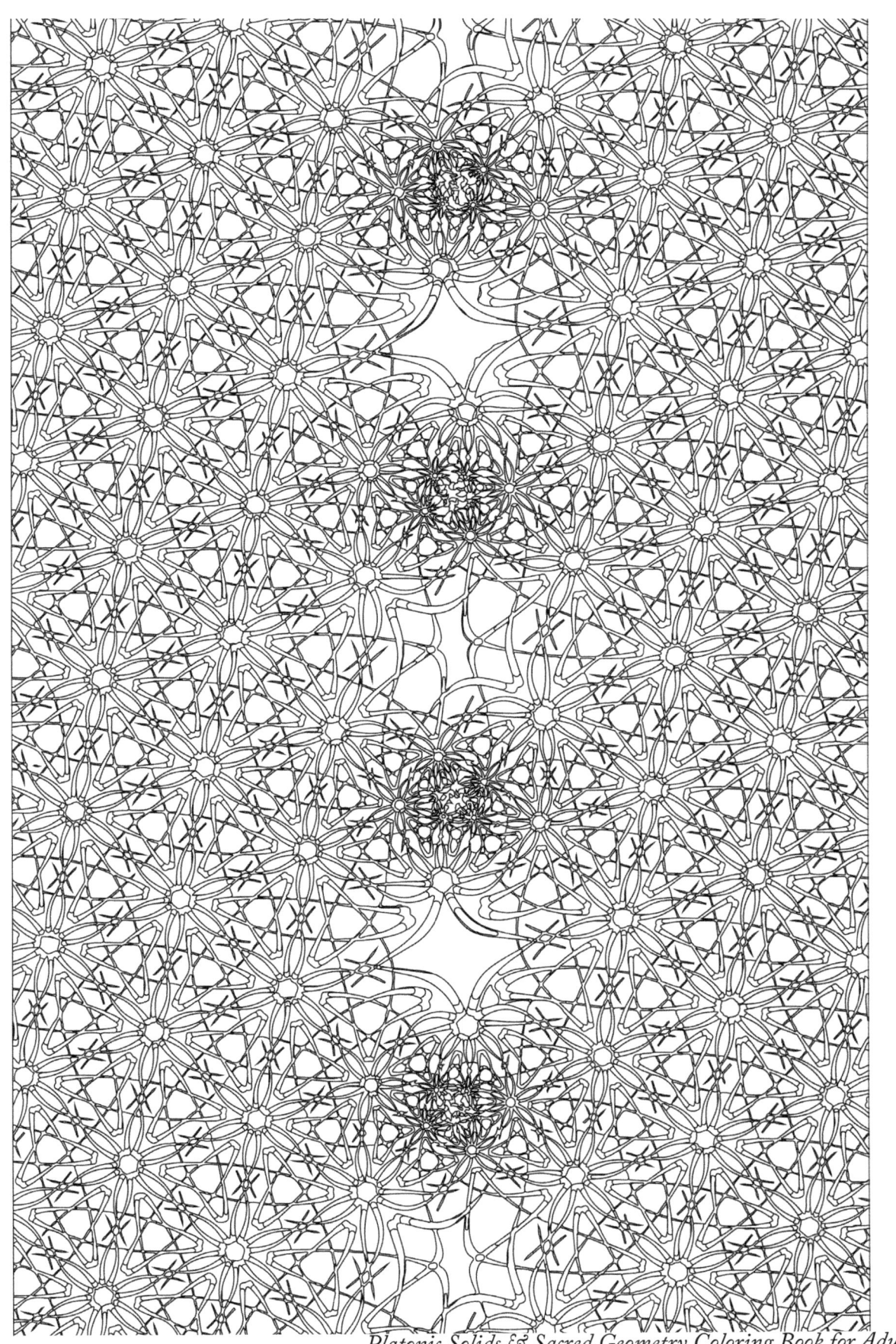

Activity 43: Order of 6

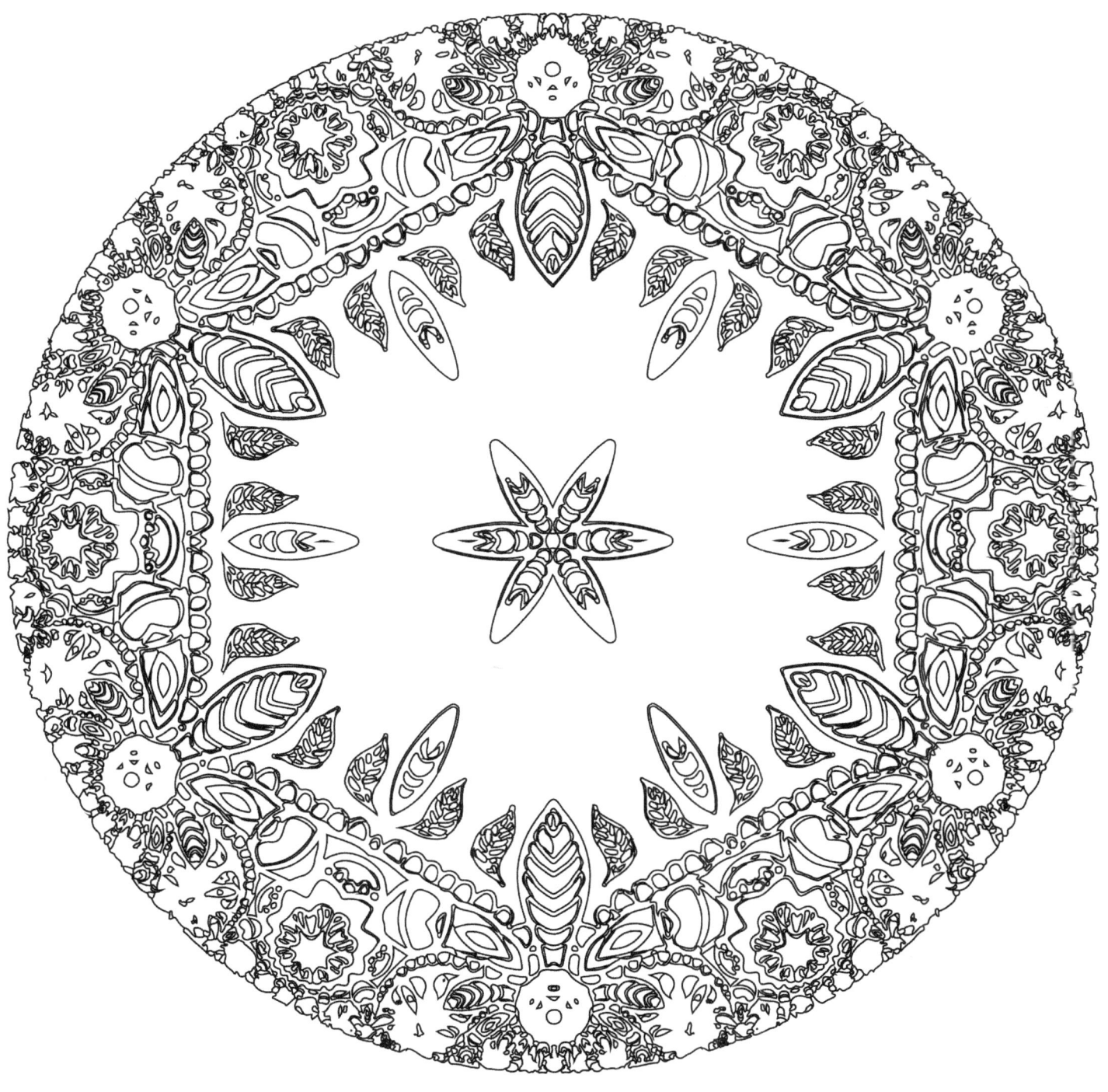

Activity 44: Lost Symbol

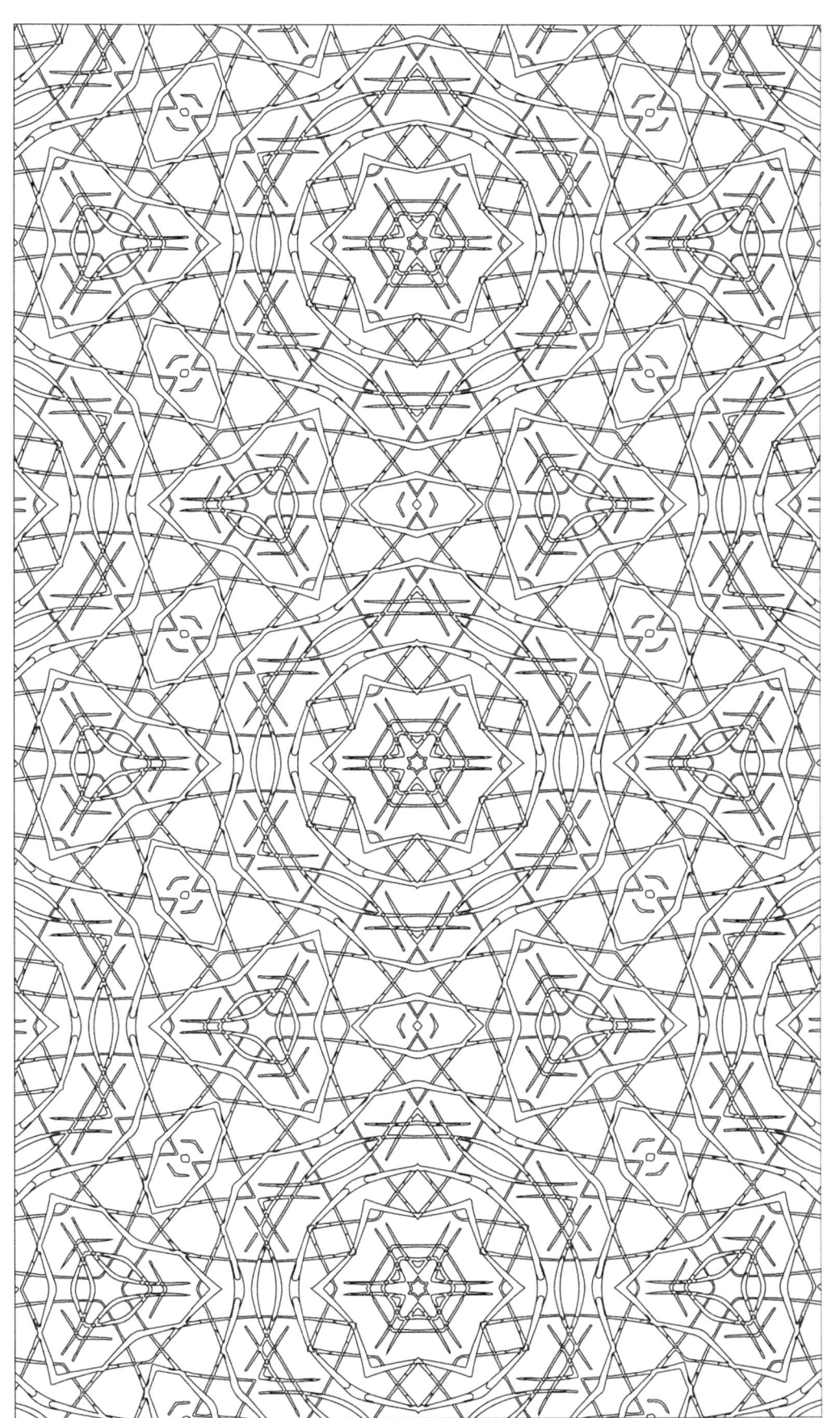

Activity 45: Triforce

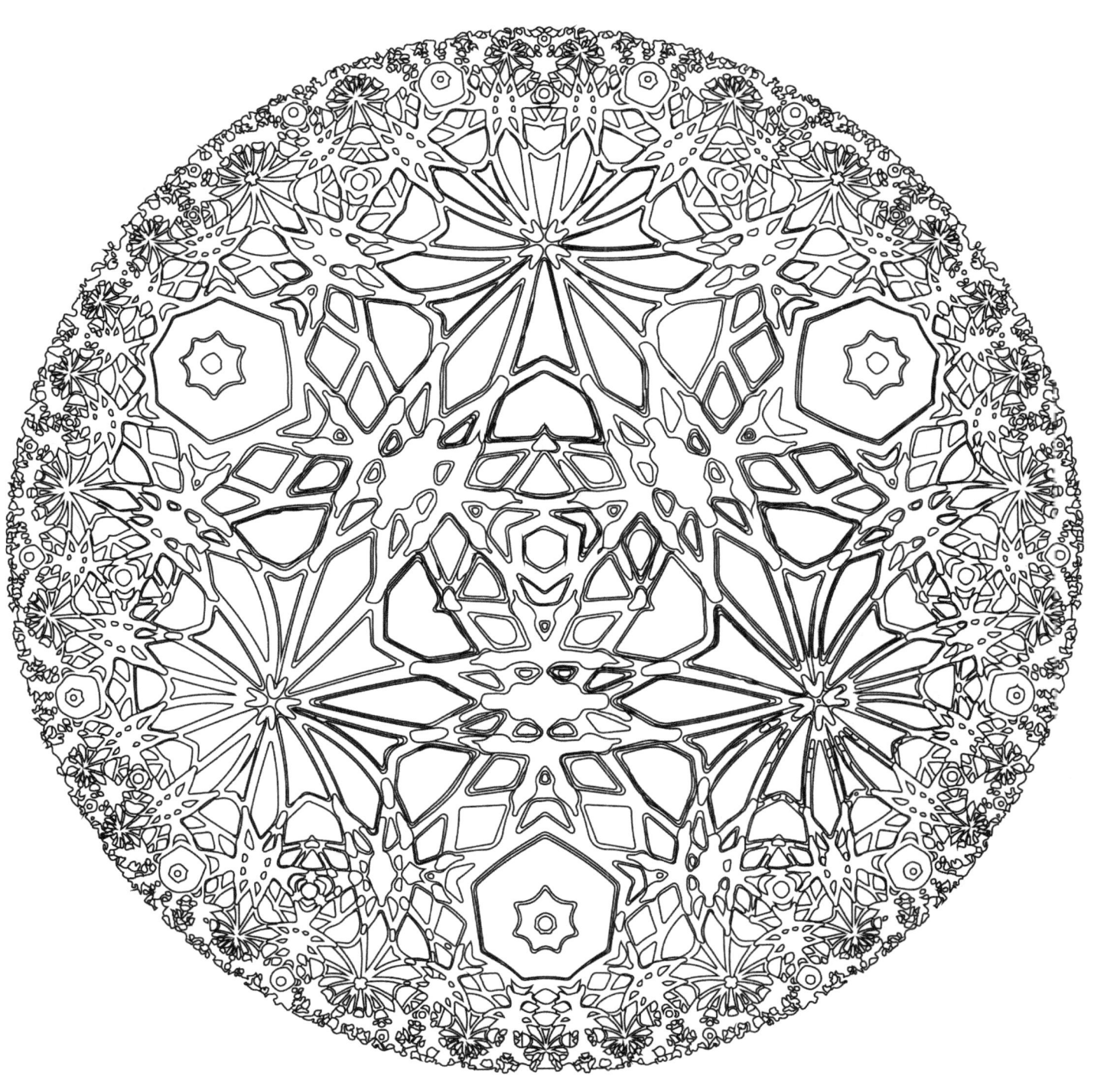

Activity 46: Frequency 528Hz

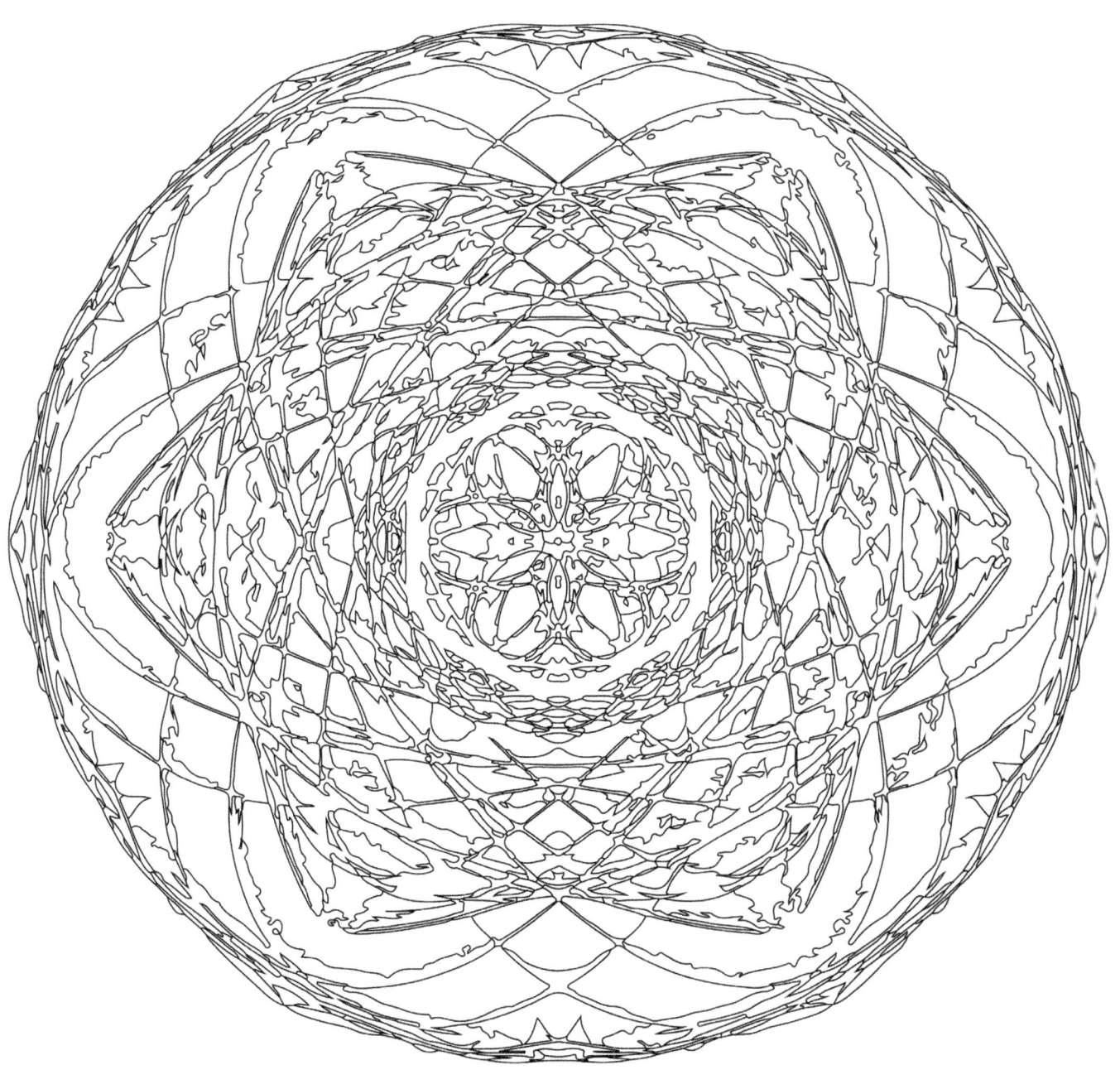

Activity 47: Minoan temple

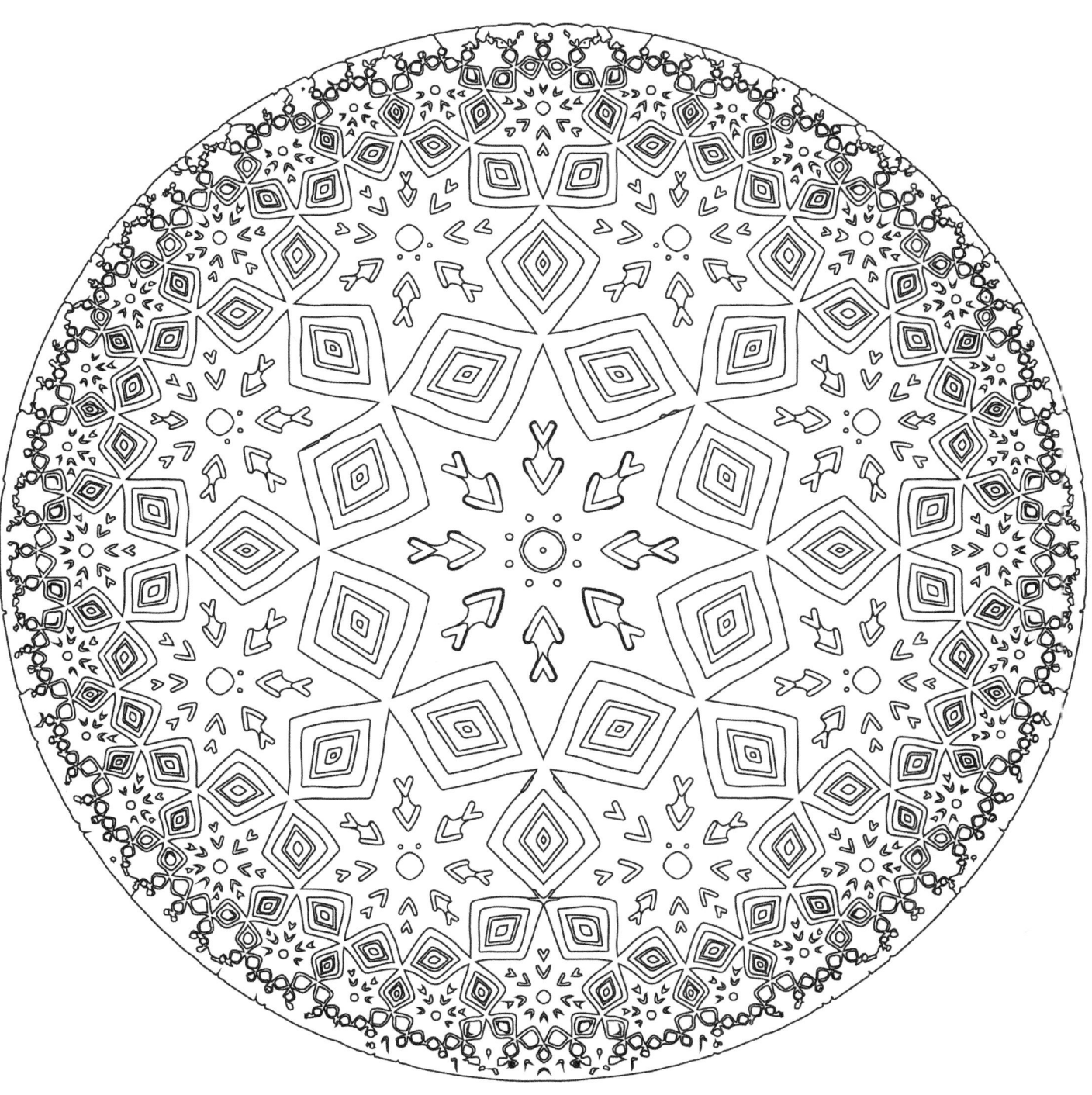

Activity 48: Flowery doodle

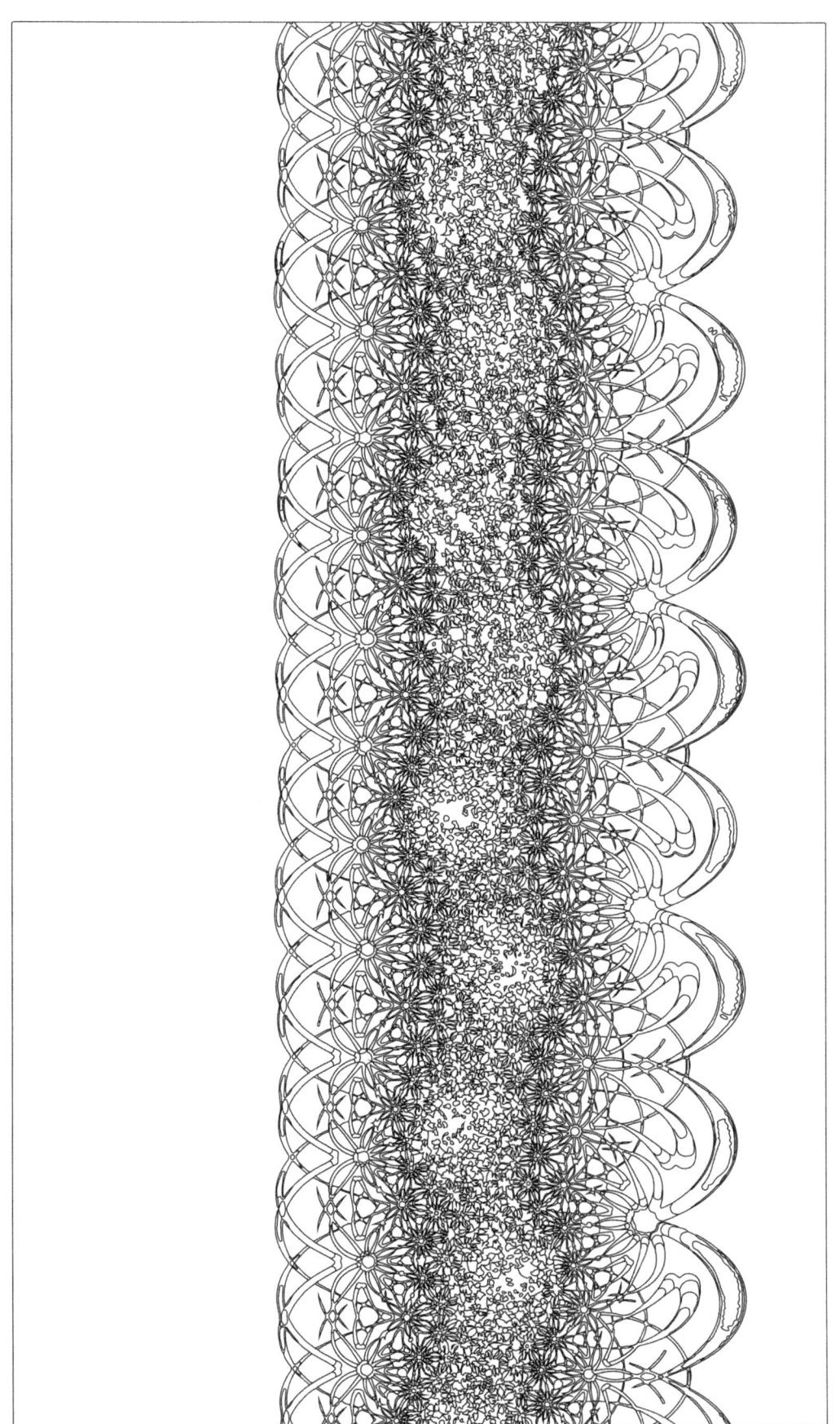

Activity 49: Ant's world

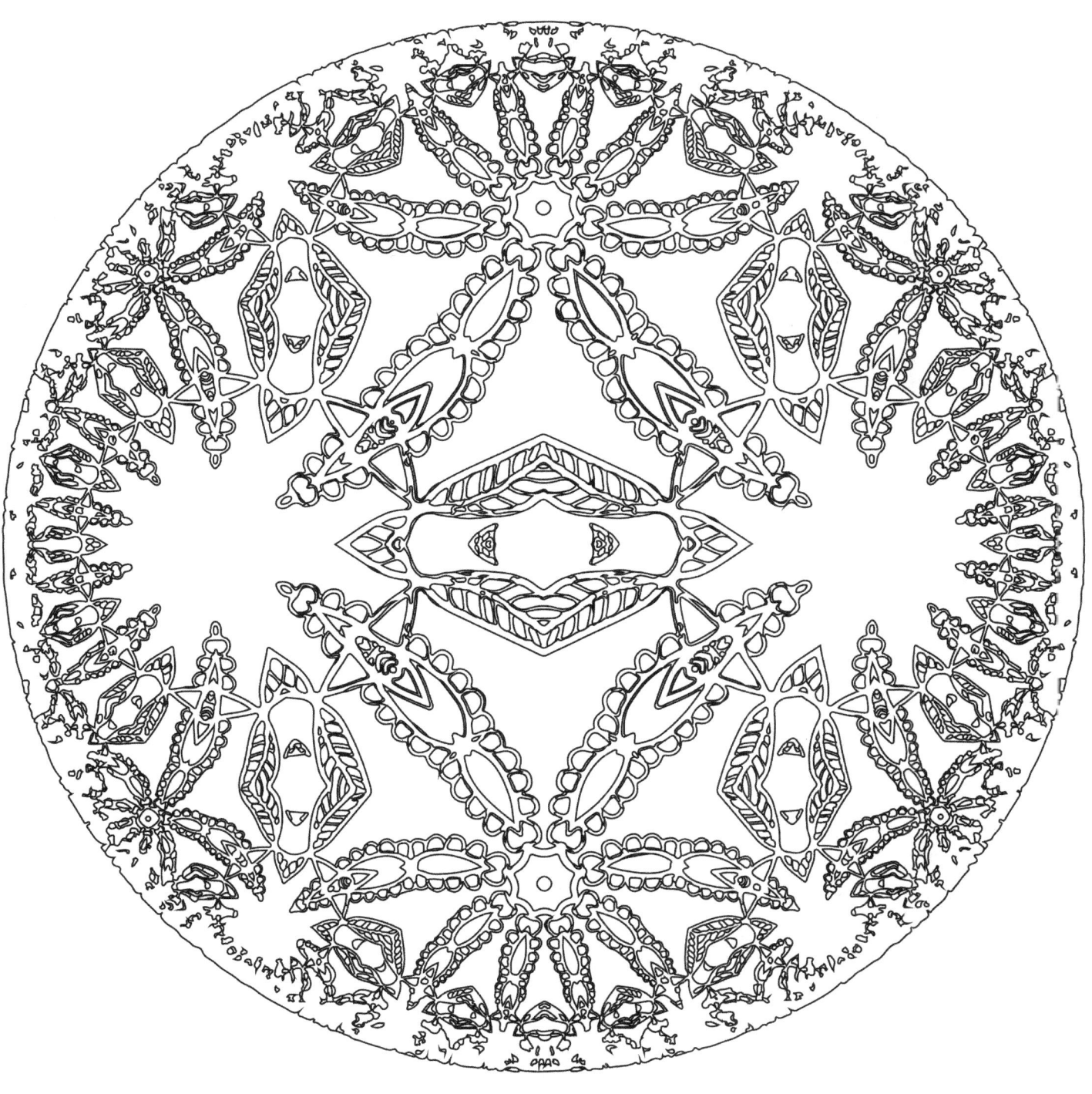

Activity 50: Universe

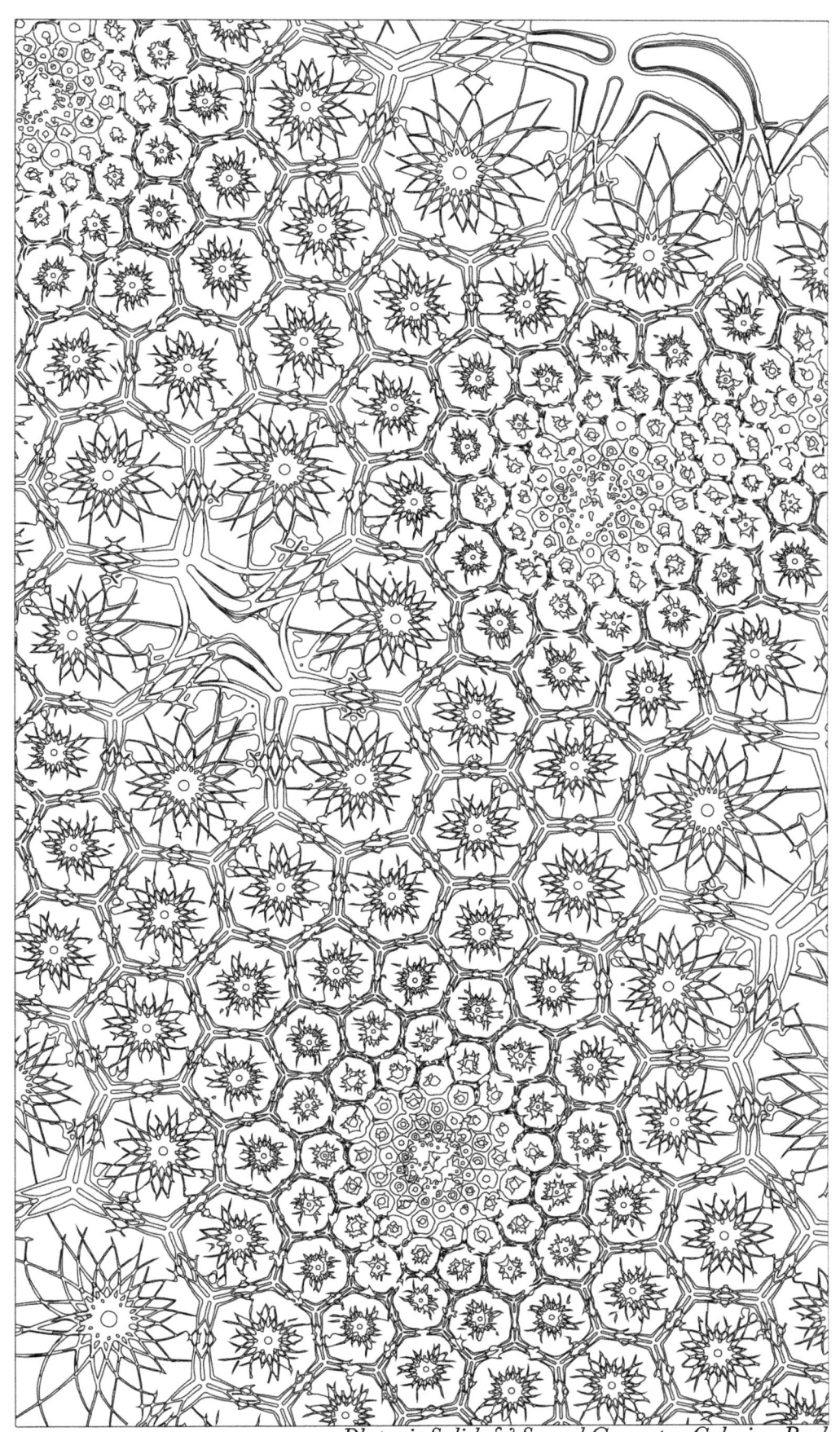

Activity 51: Aztec Calendar

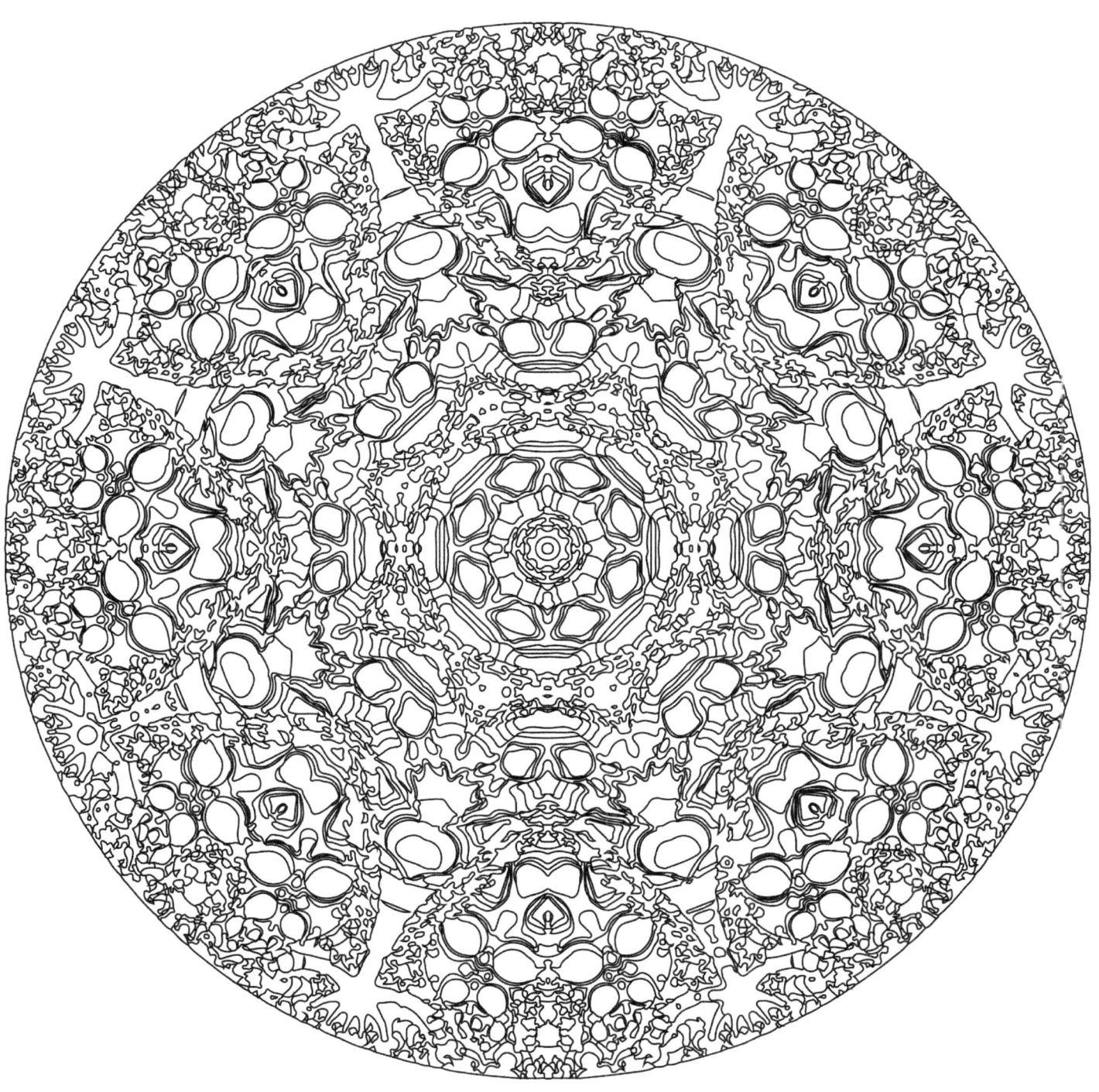

Activity 52: Alien messege

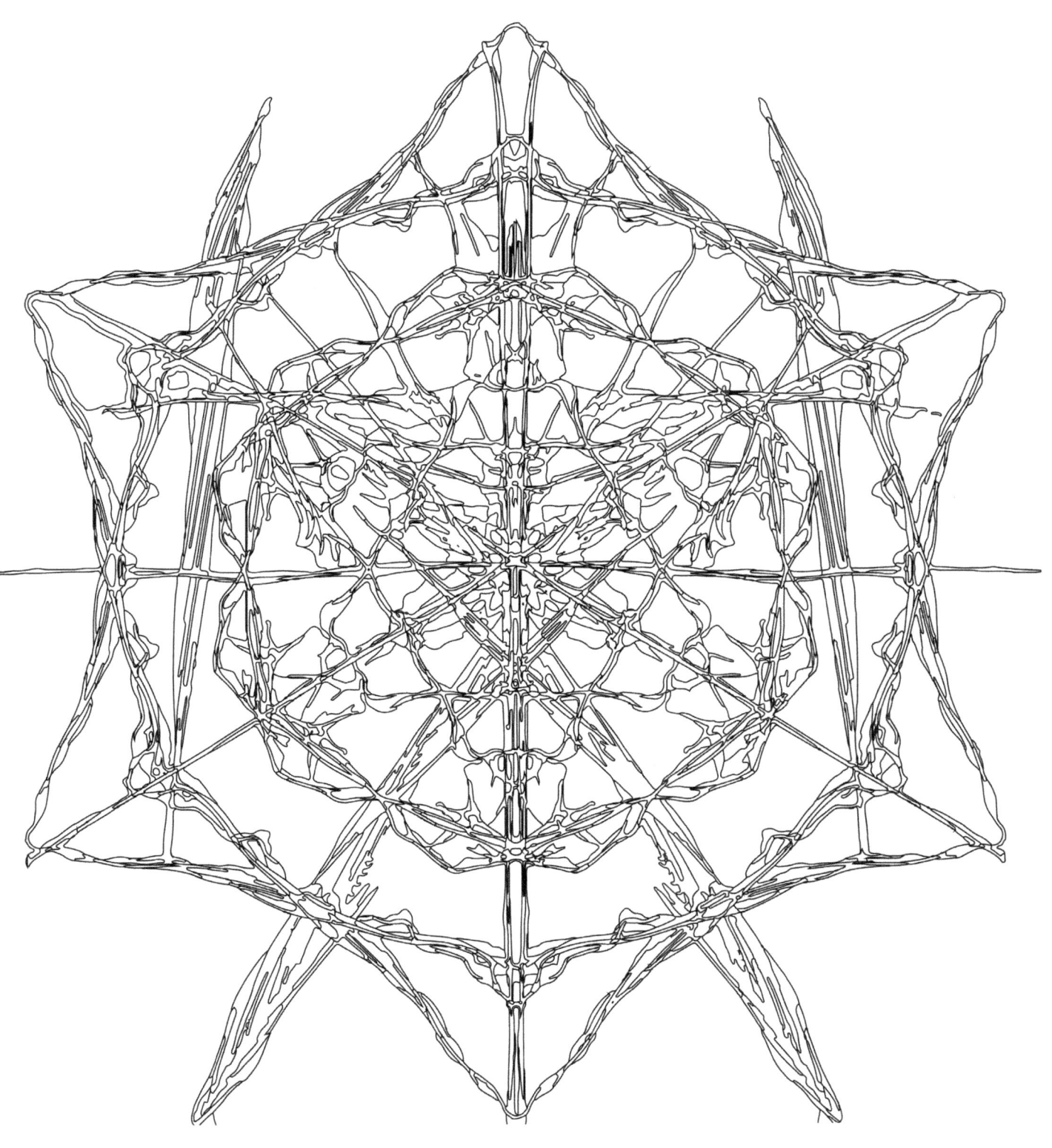

Activity 53: Celestial

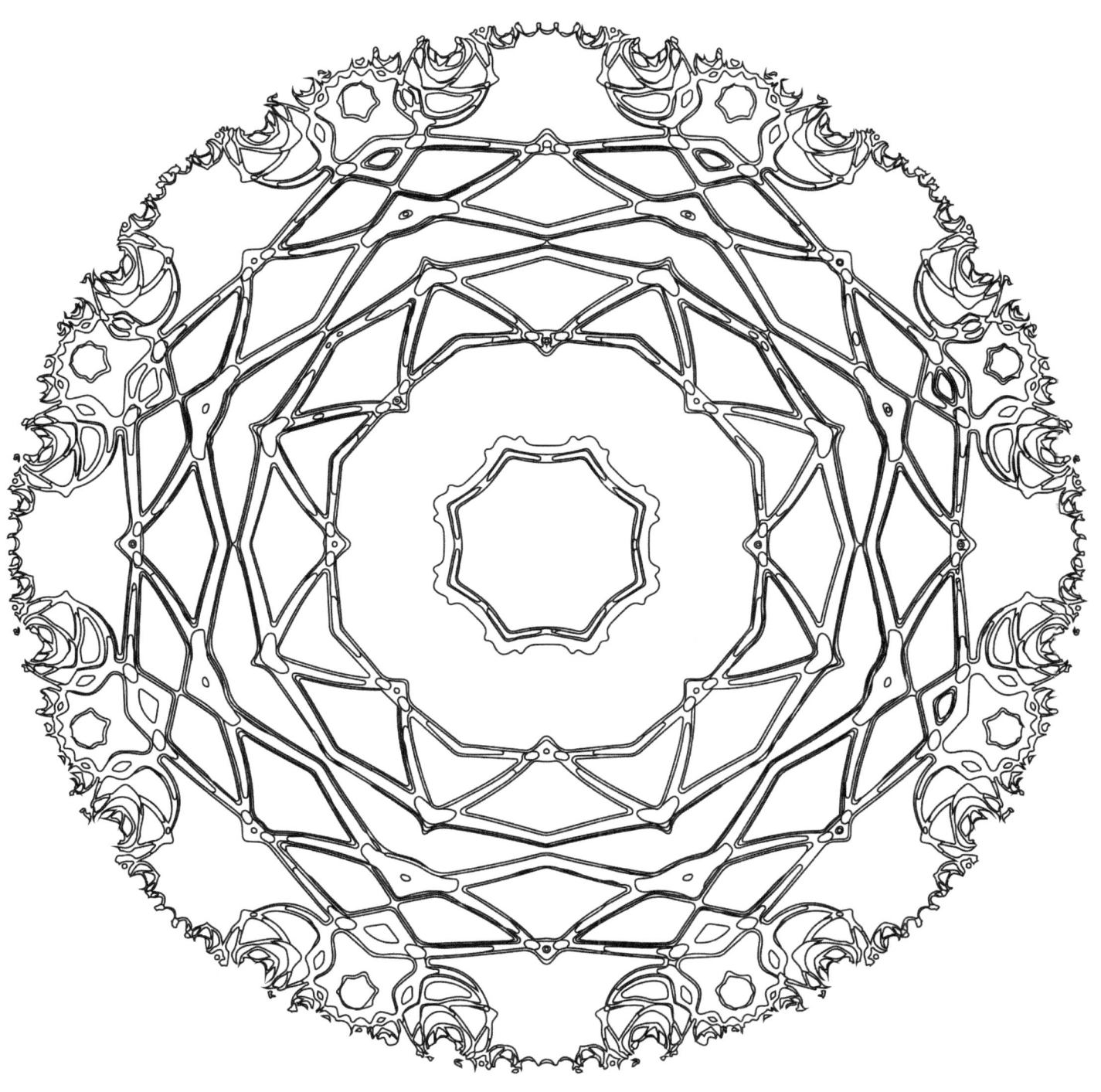

Activity 54: Arc Reactor

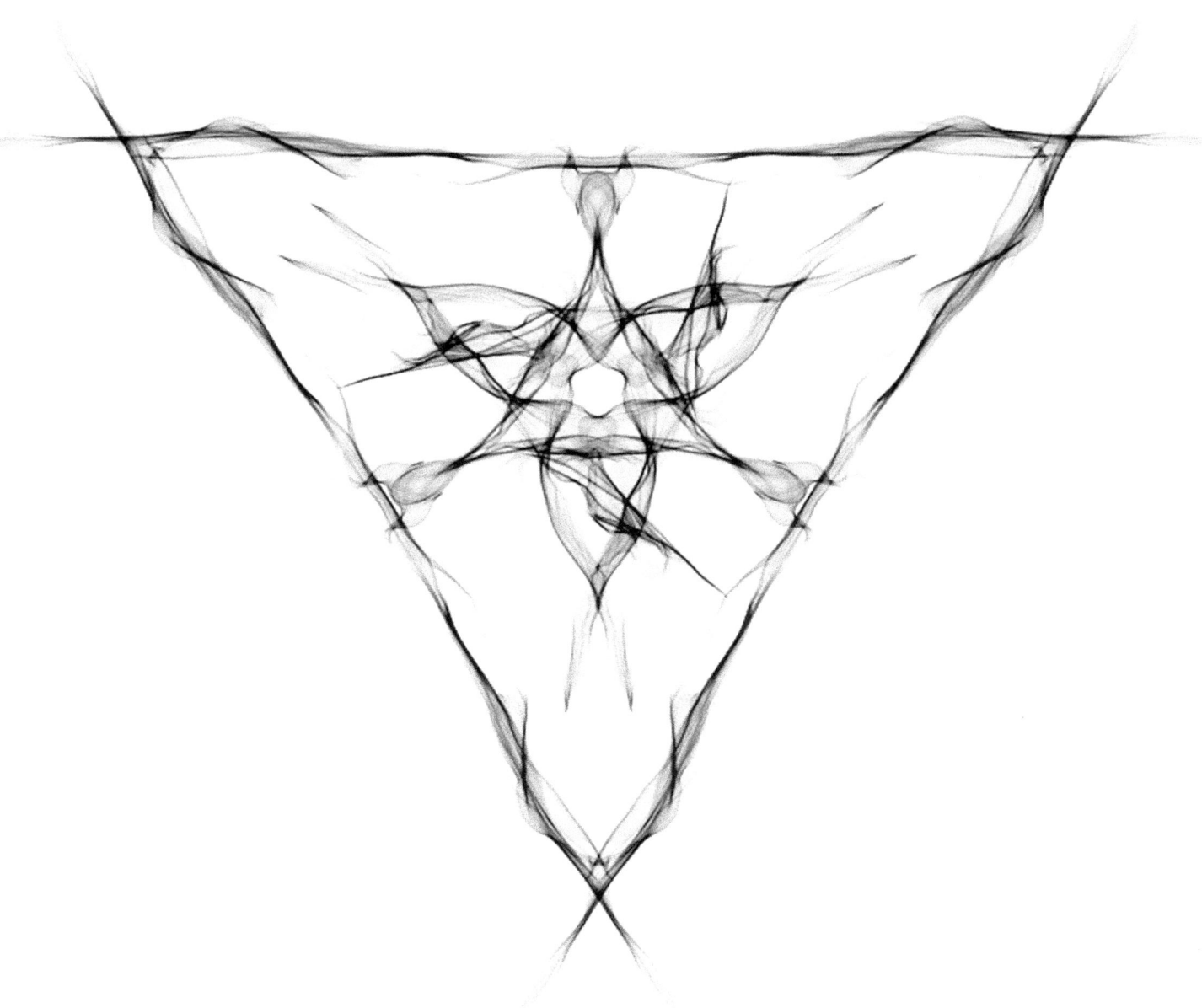

Activity 55: Complexity

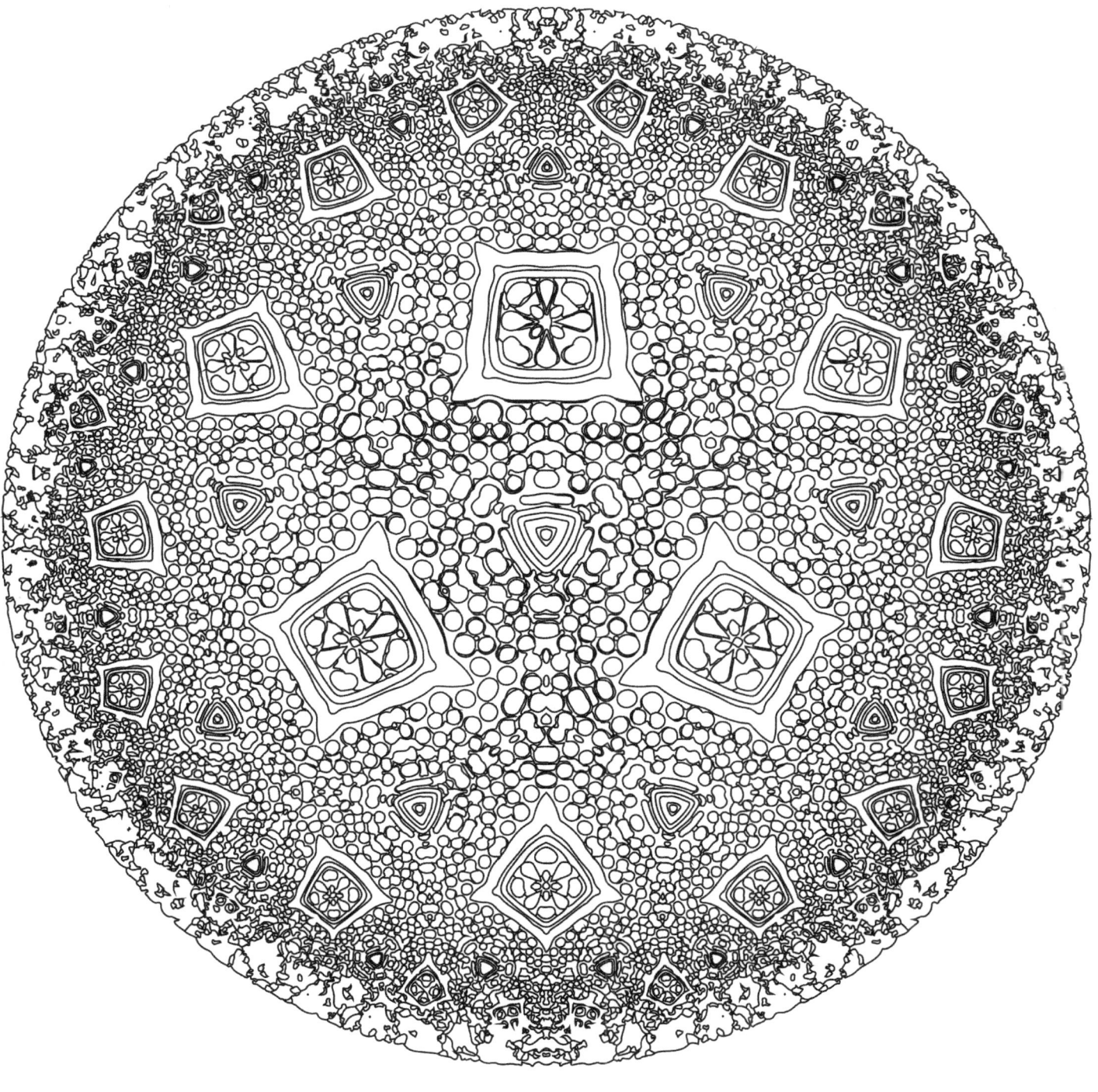

Activity 56: Free Energy

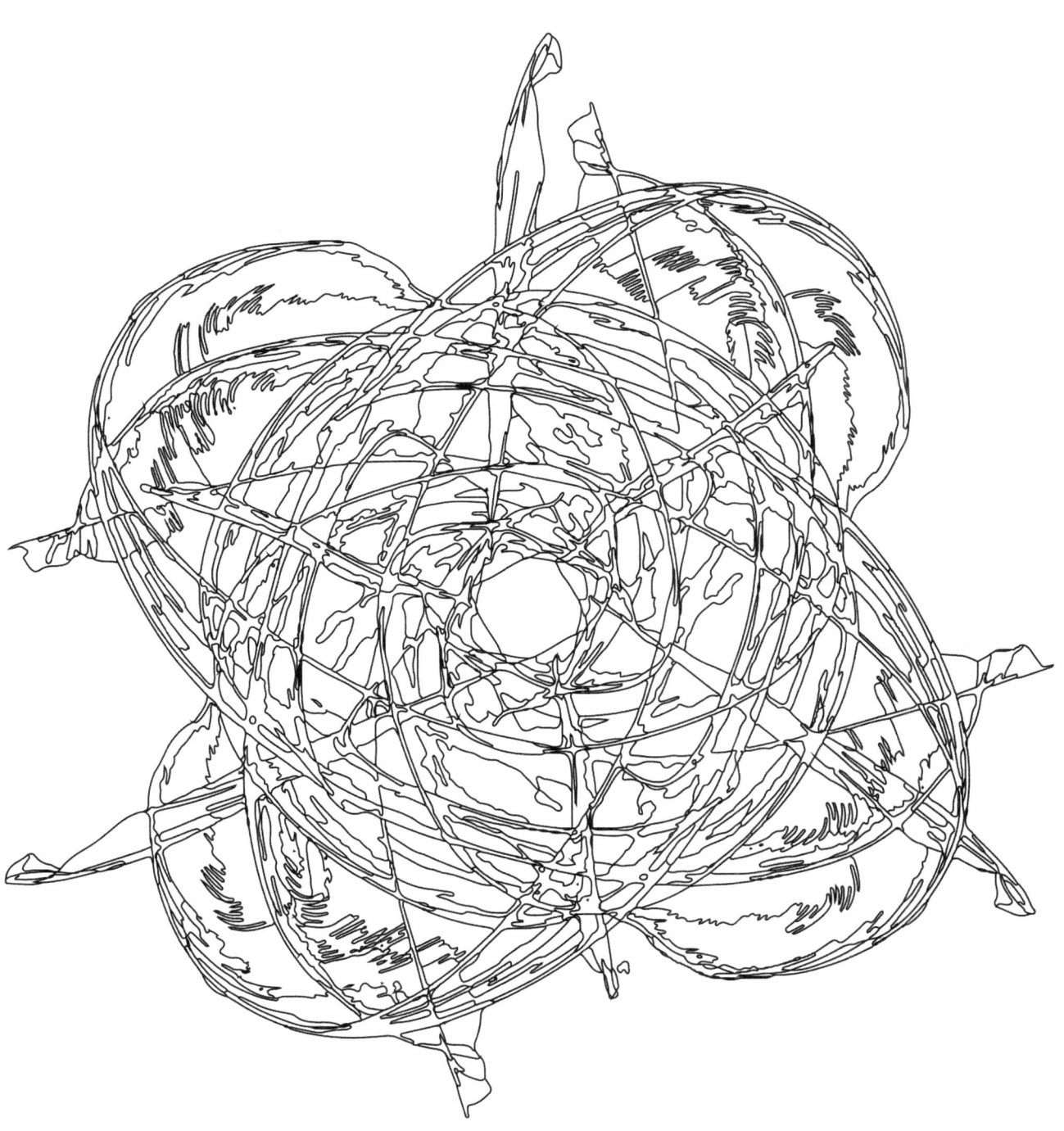

Activity 57: Electron reactor

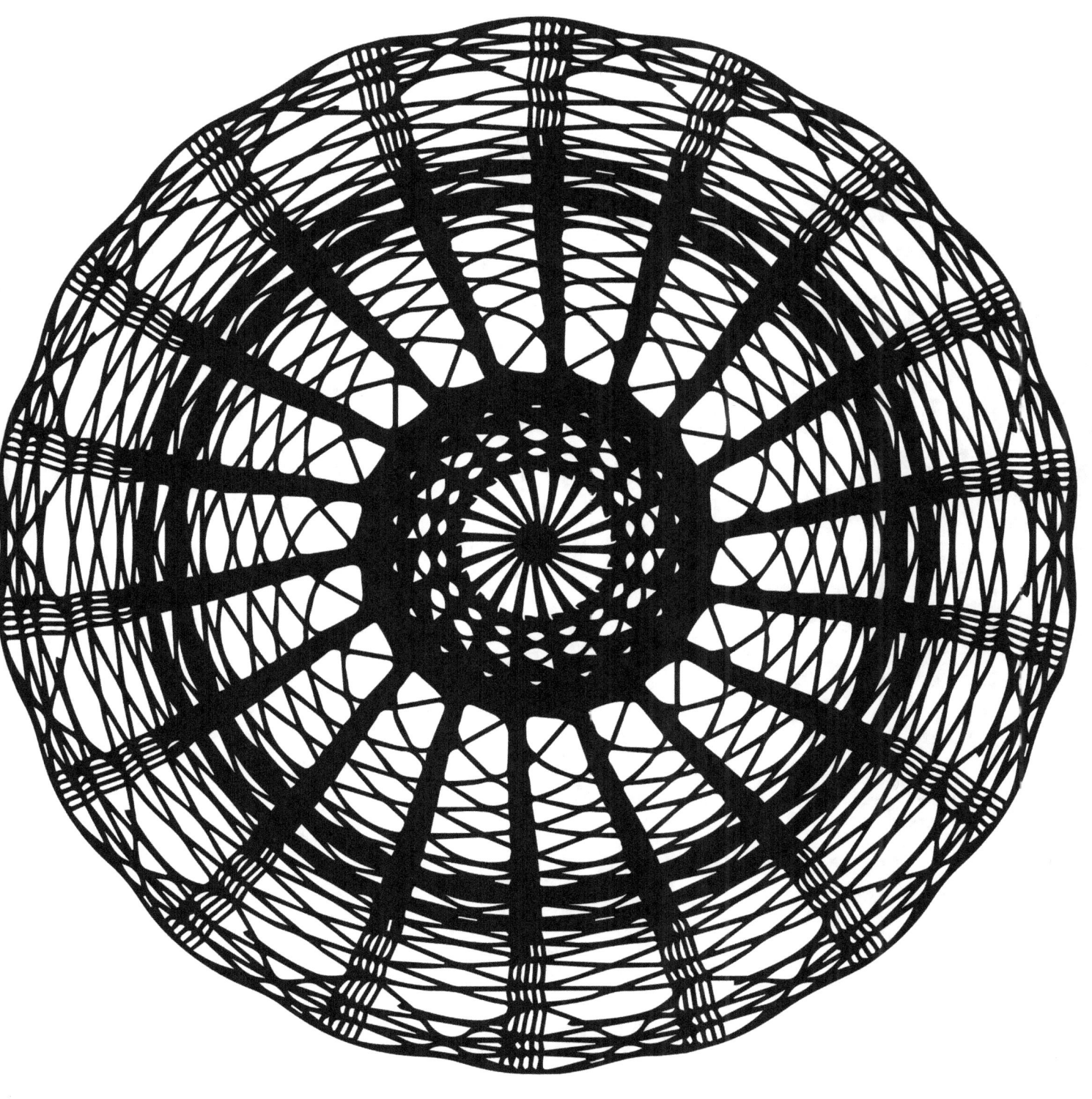

Activity 58: Musical colors

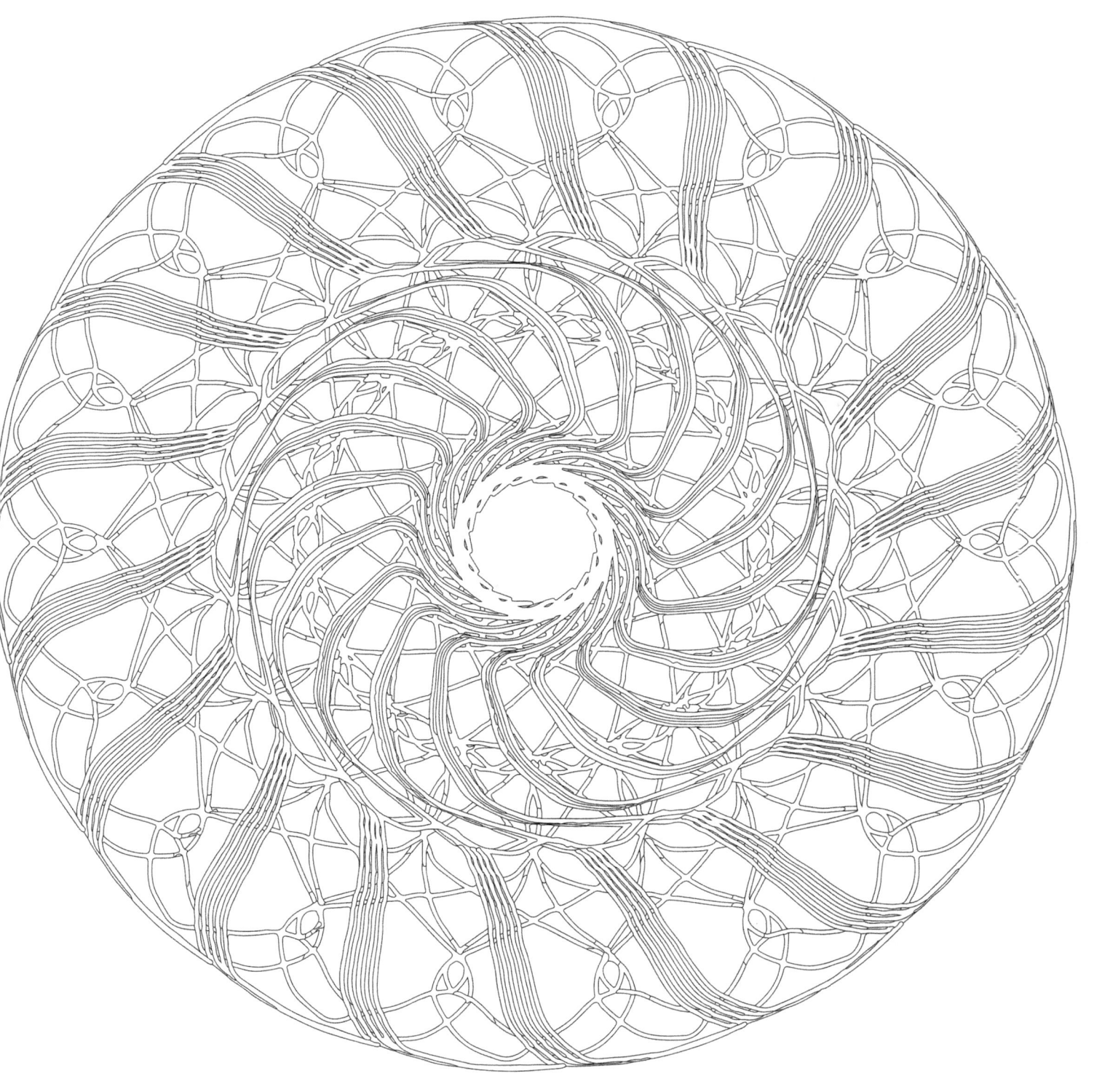

Activity 59: Arcade

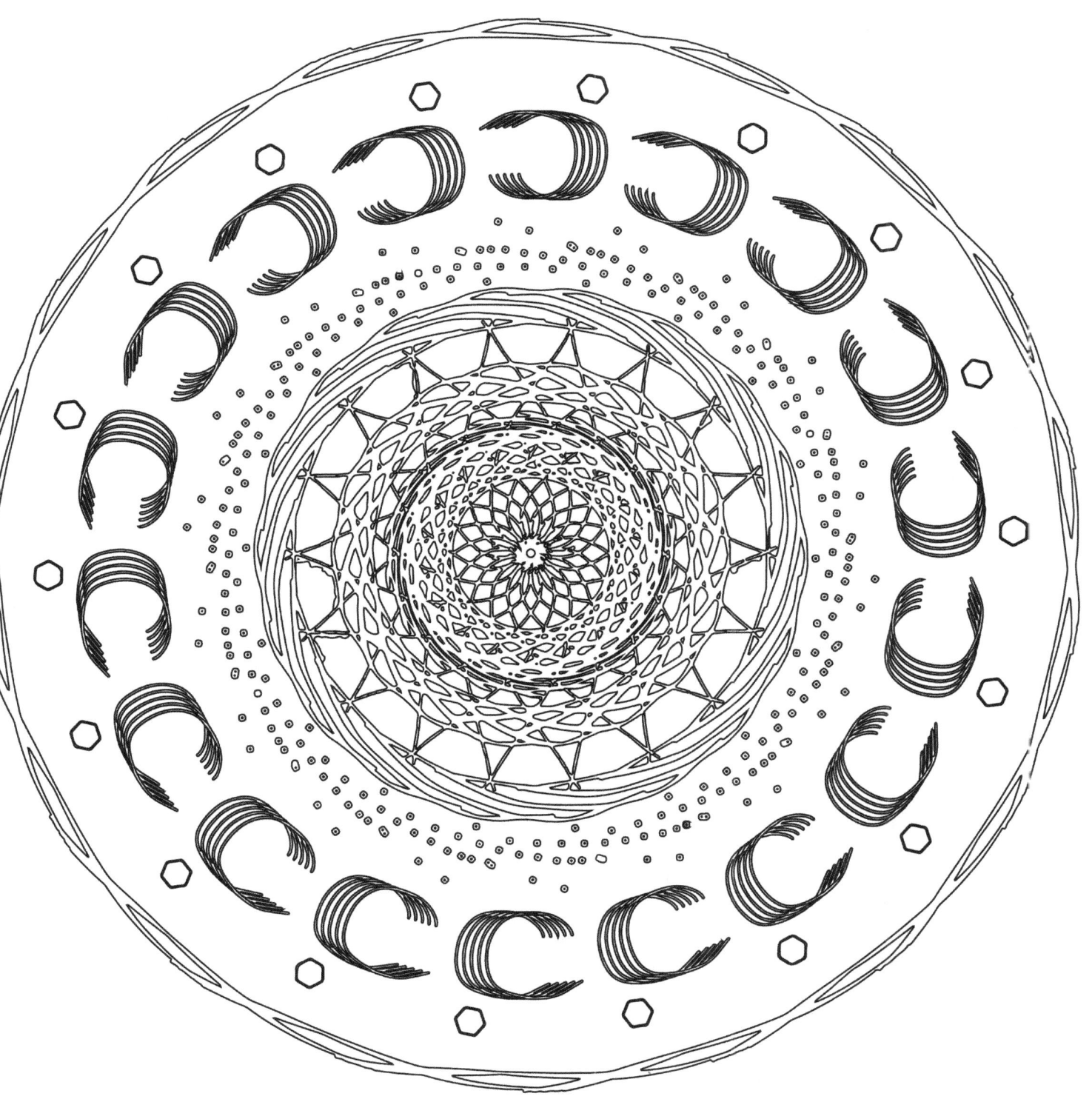

Activity 60: Spiritual path

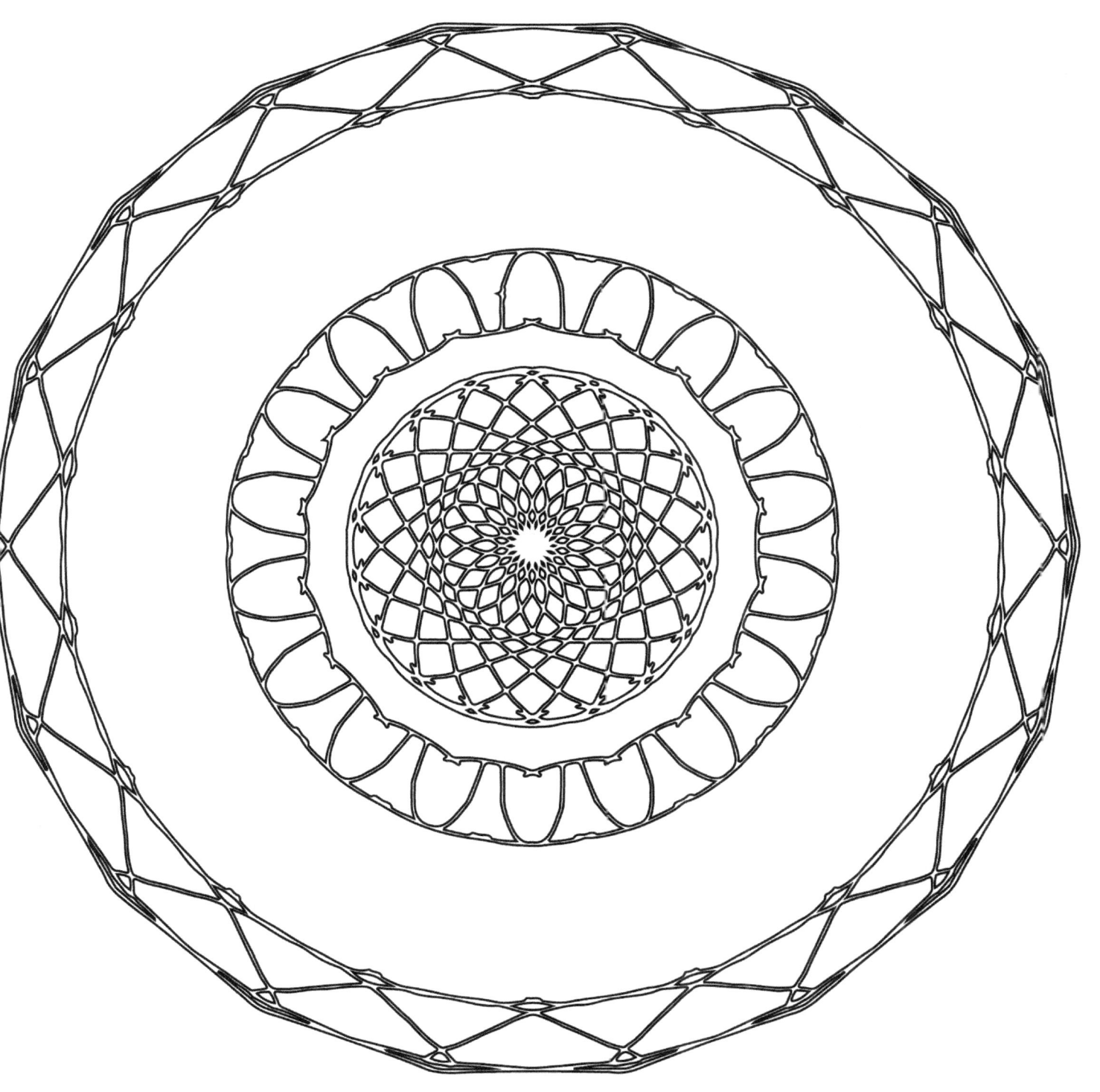

Activity 61: Alpha centauri

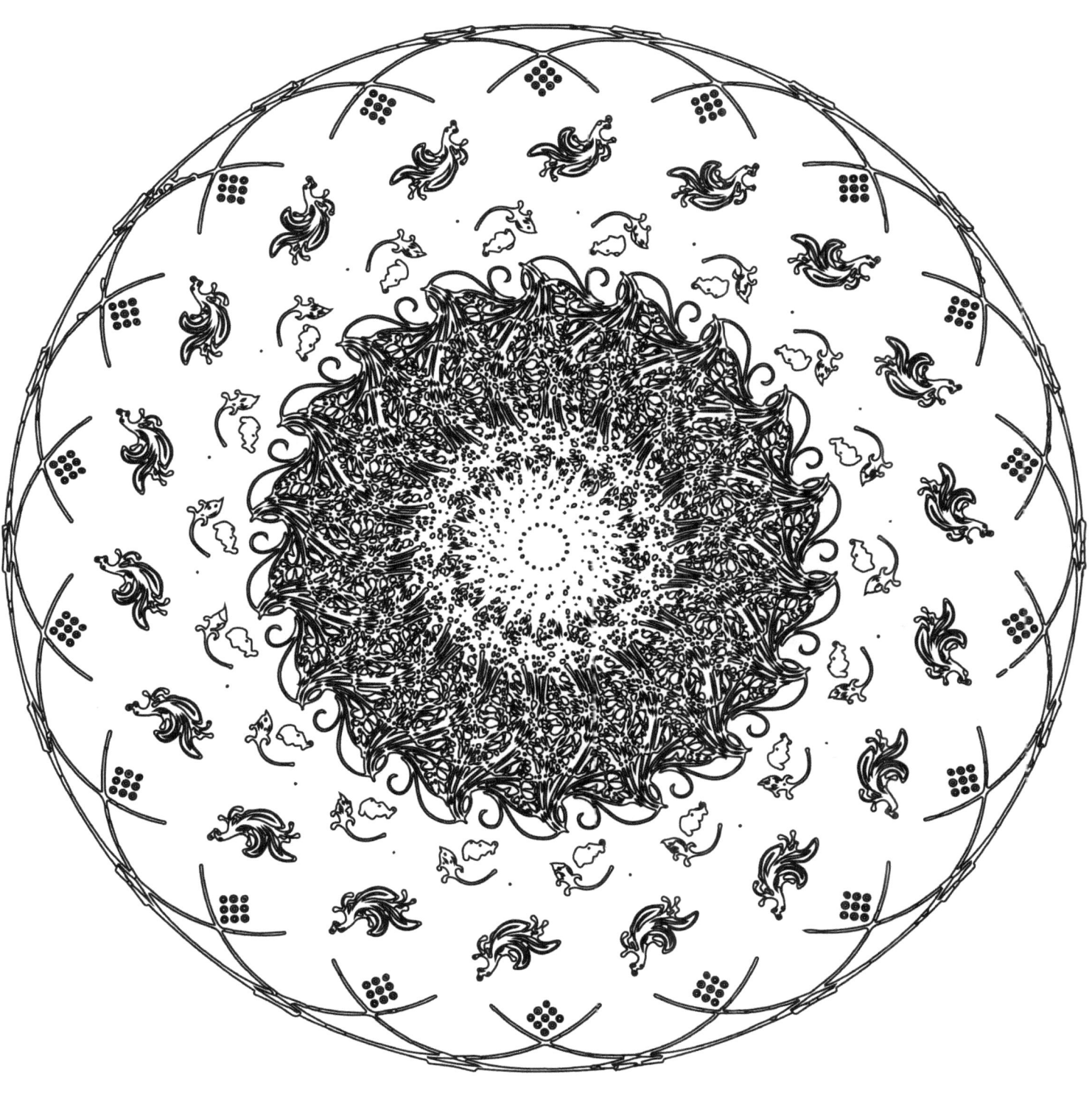

Activity 62: Key to Lothlorien

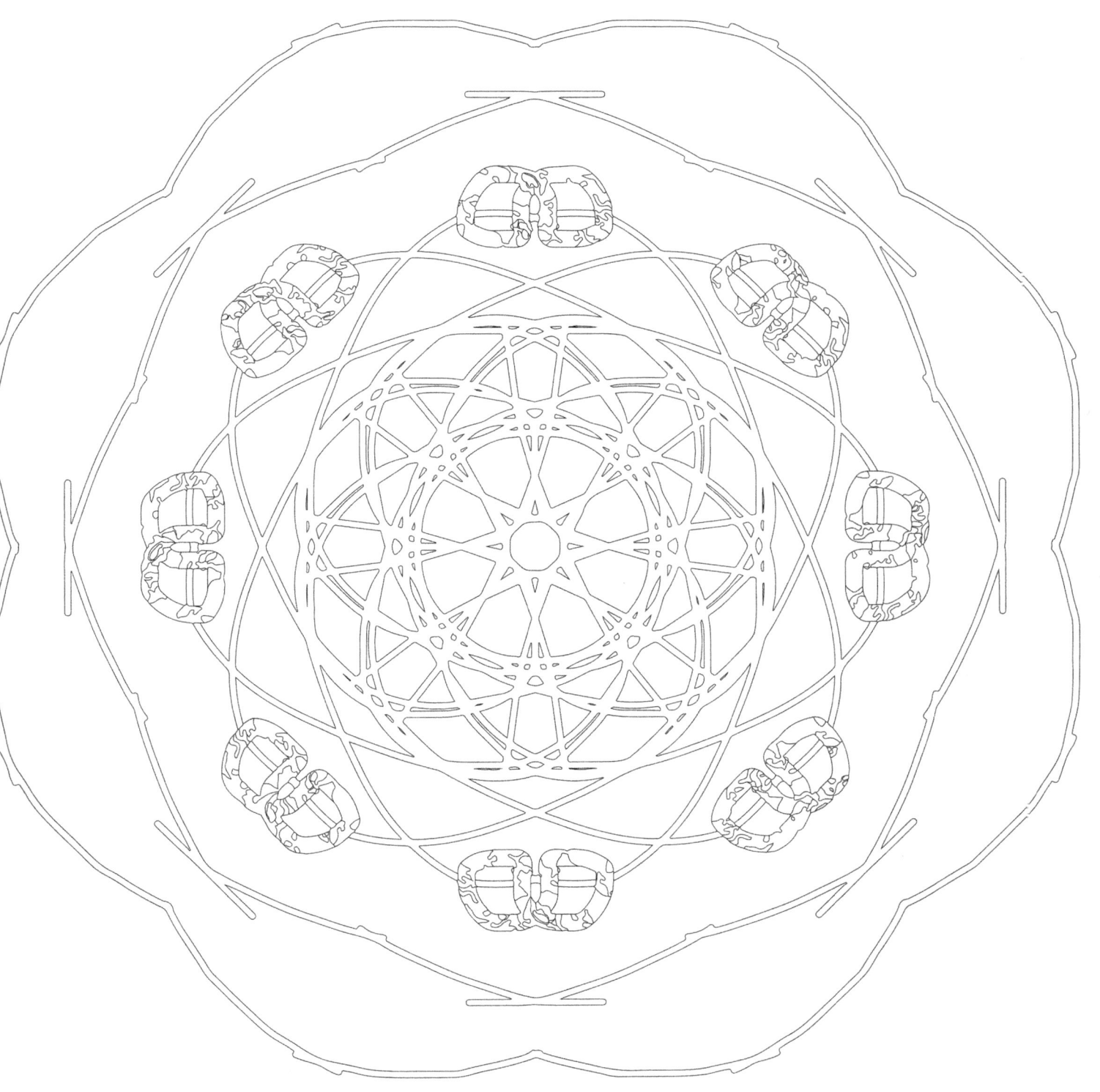

Platonic Solids & Sacred Geometry Coloring Book for Adults

Activity 63: Path to Nirvana

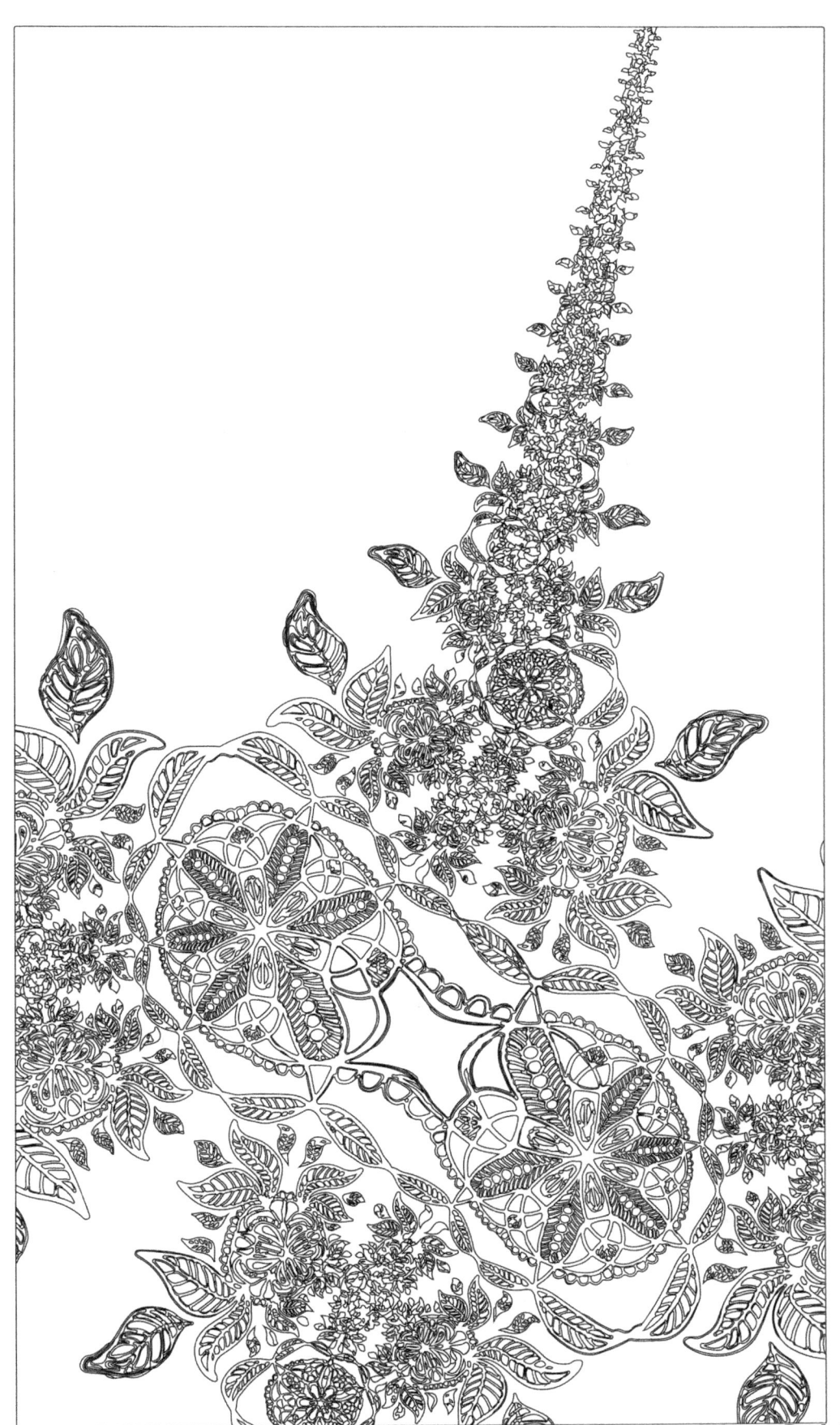

Activity 64: Spider web

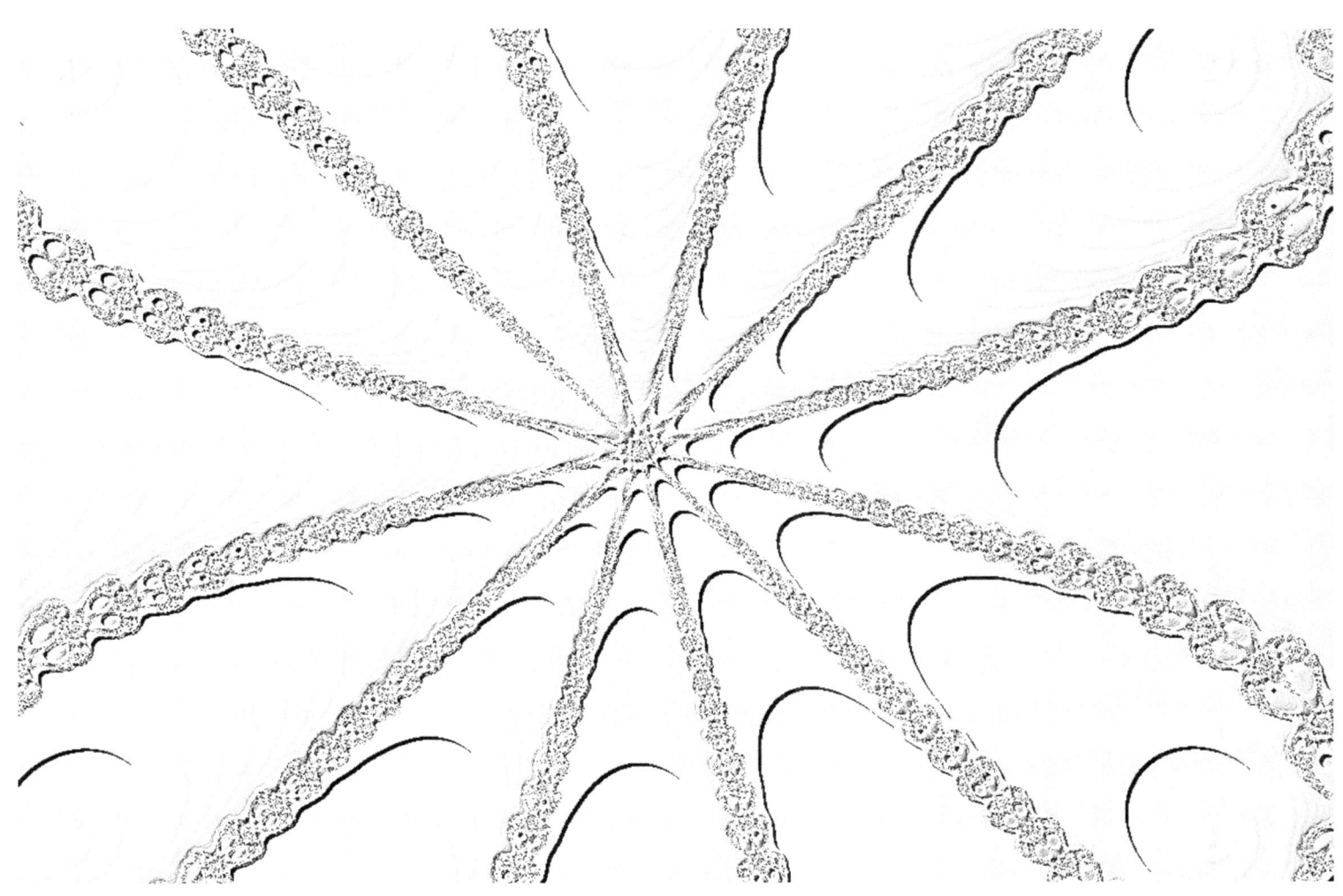

Activity 65: Heavenly light

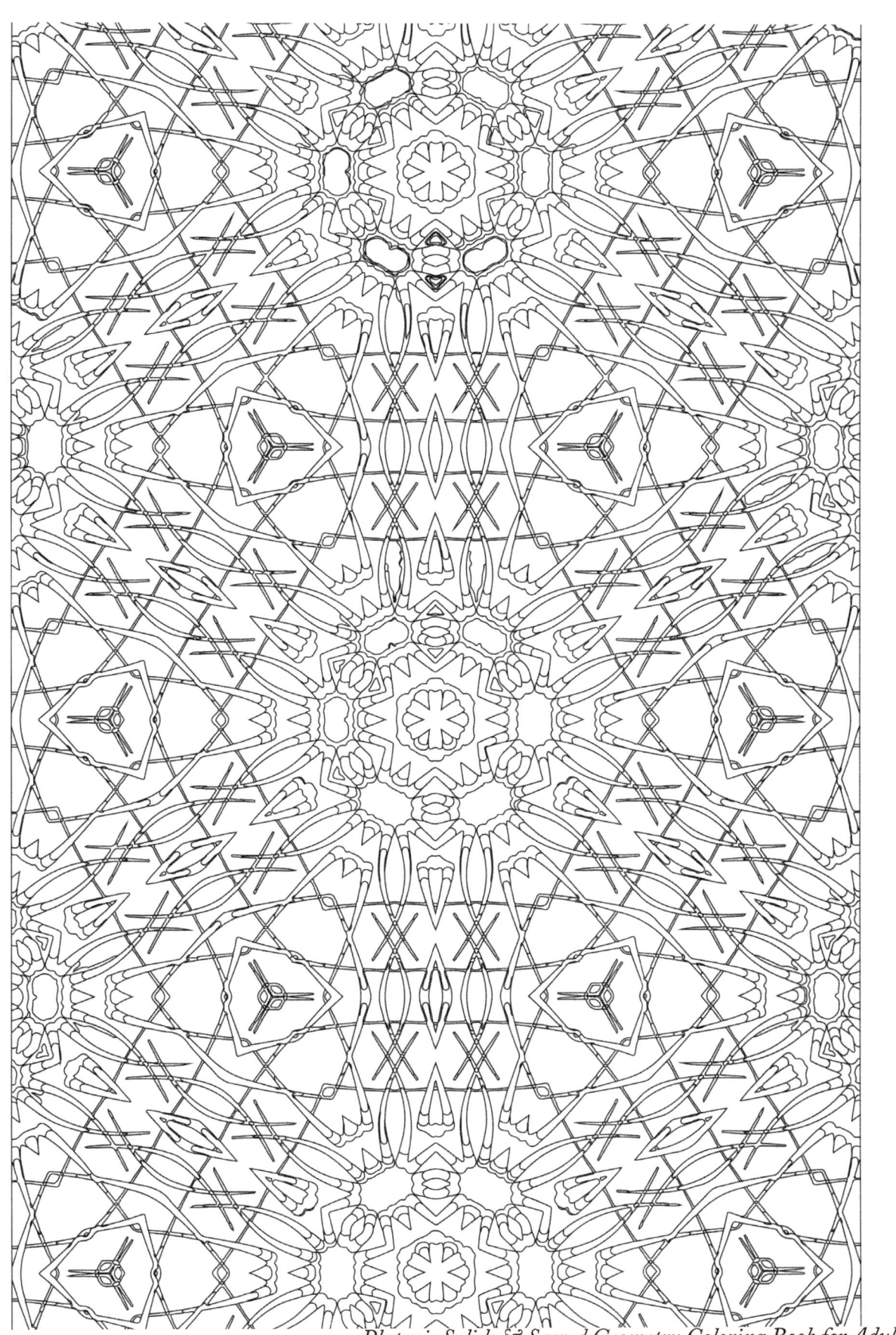

Activity 66: Theta - phi

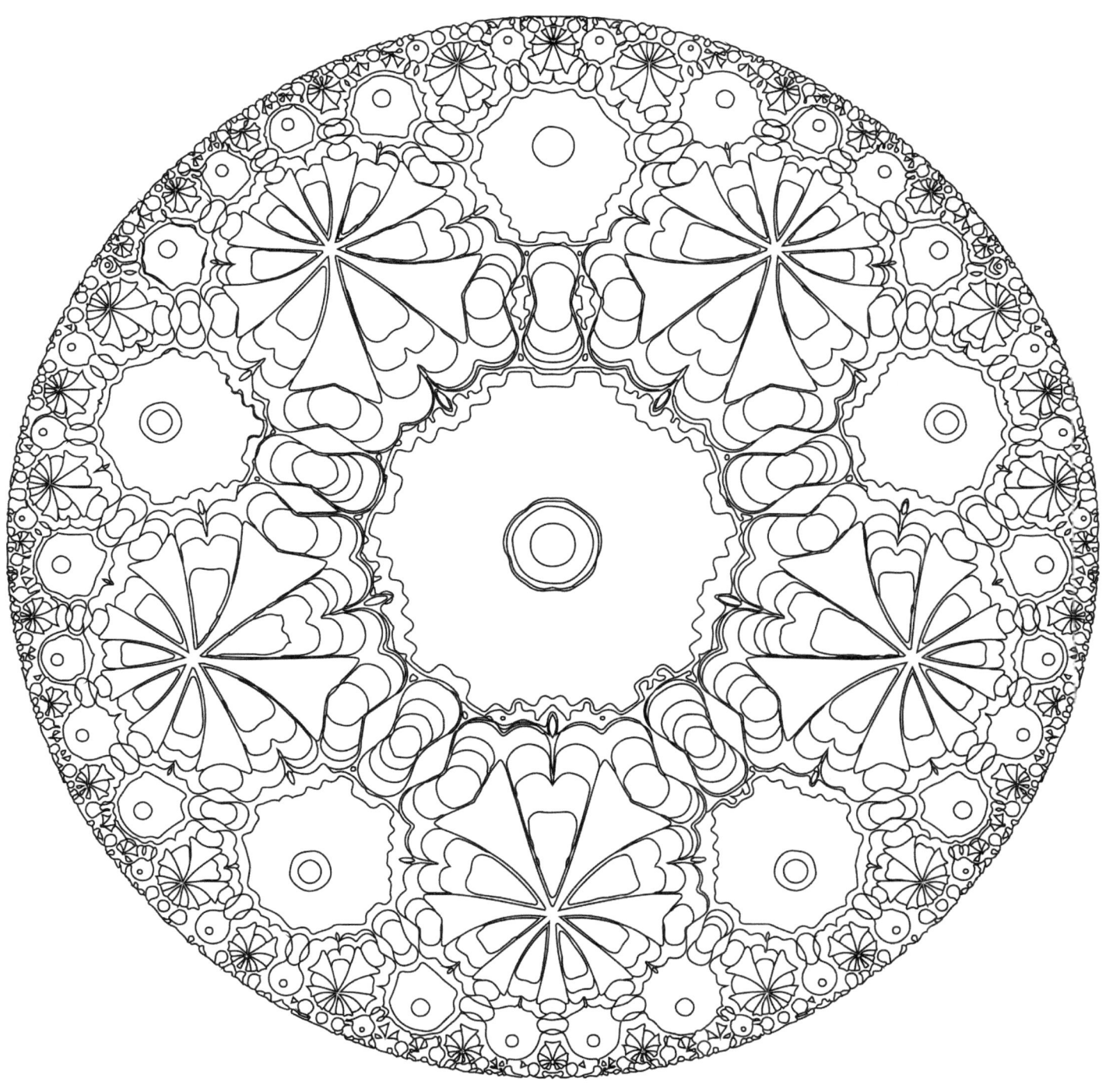

Activity 67: Cathedral

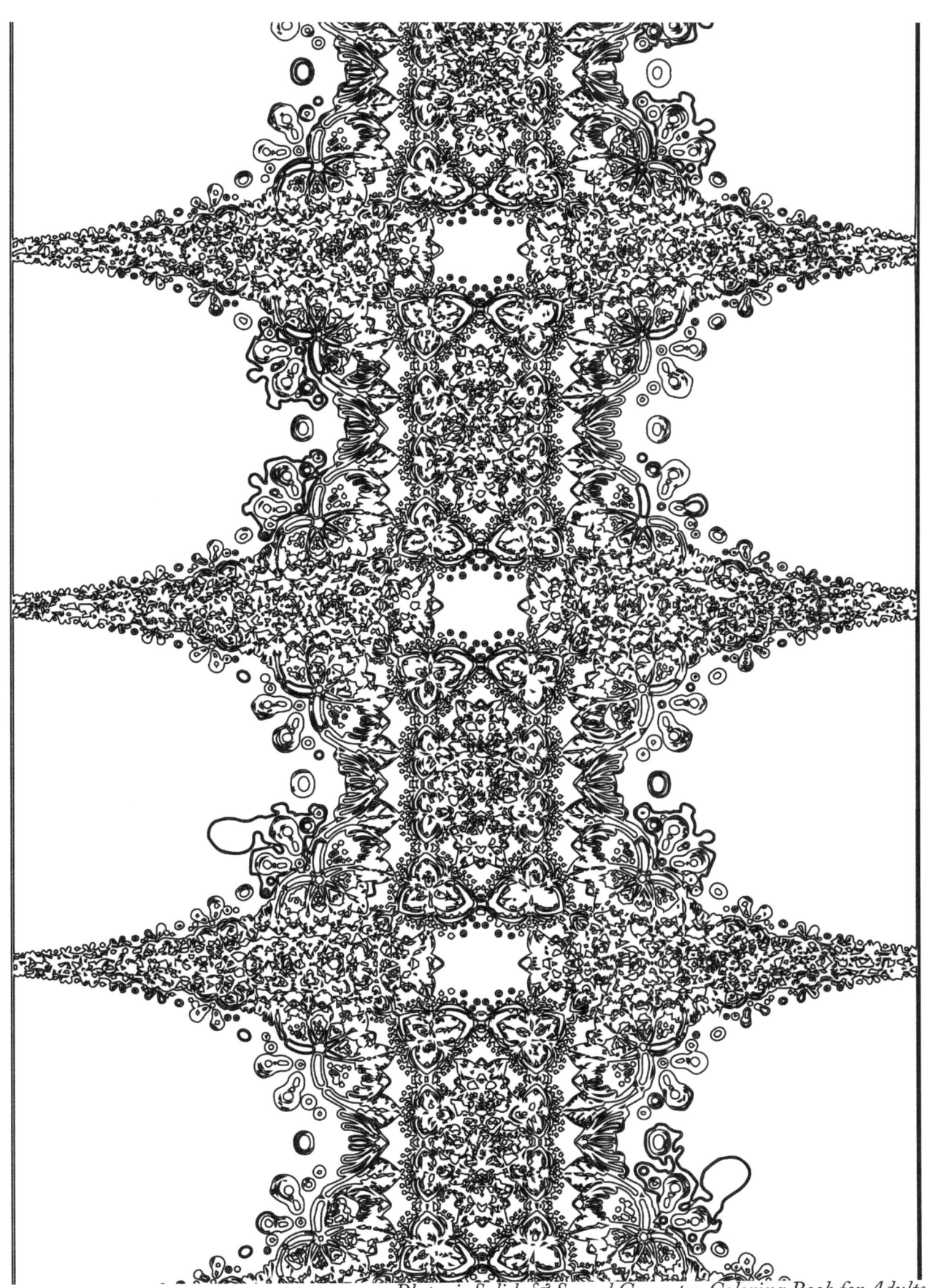

Activity 68: Pastoral symphony

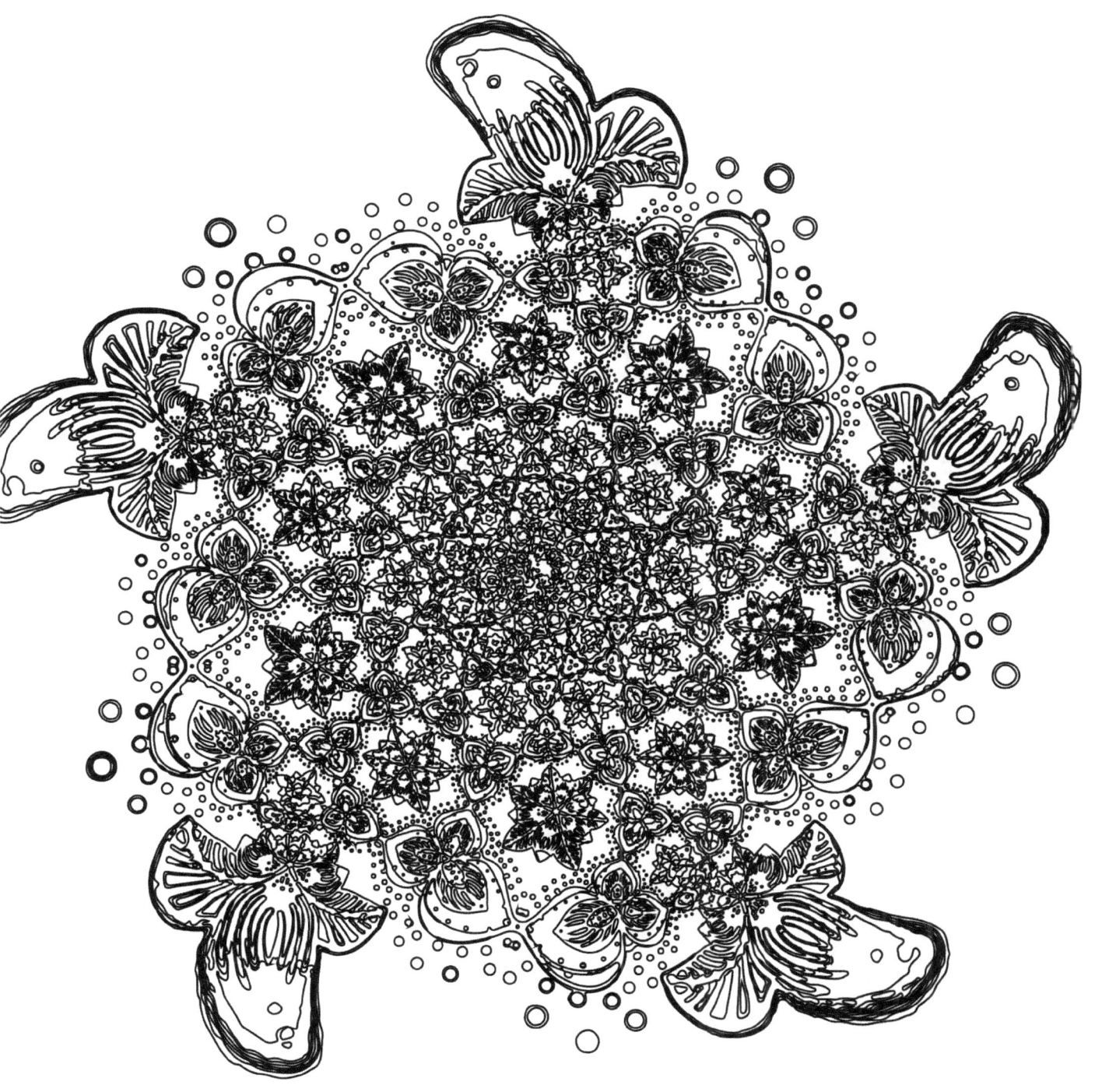

Activity 69: Hare Krishna

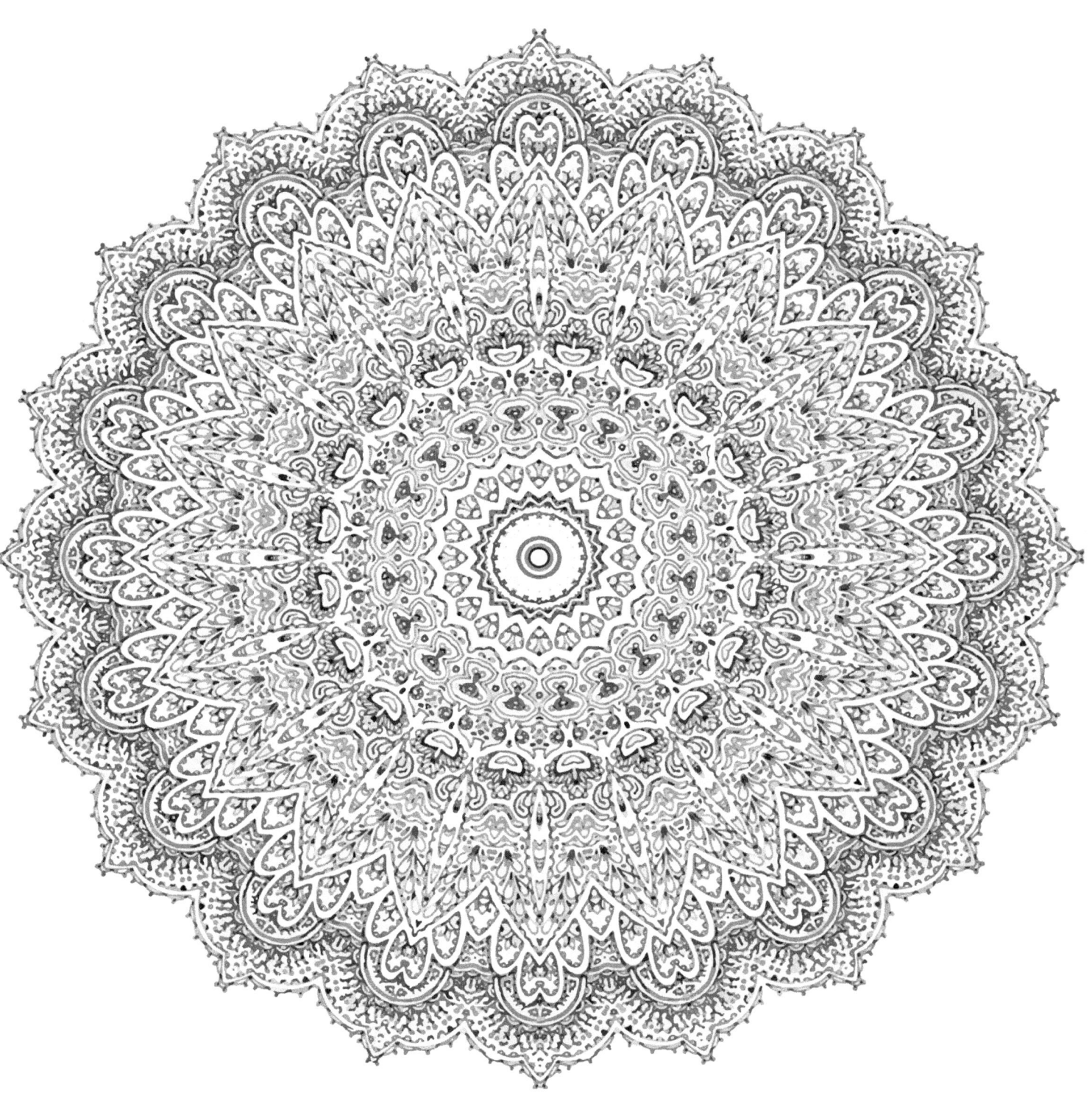

Activity 70: Centripetal force

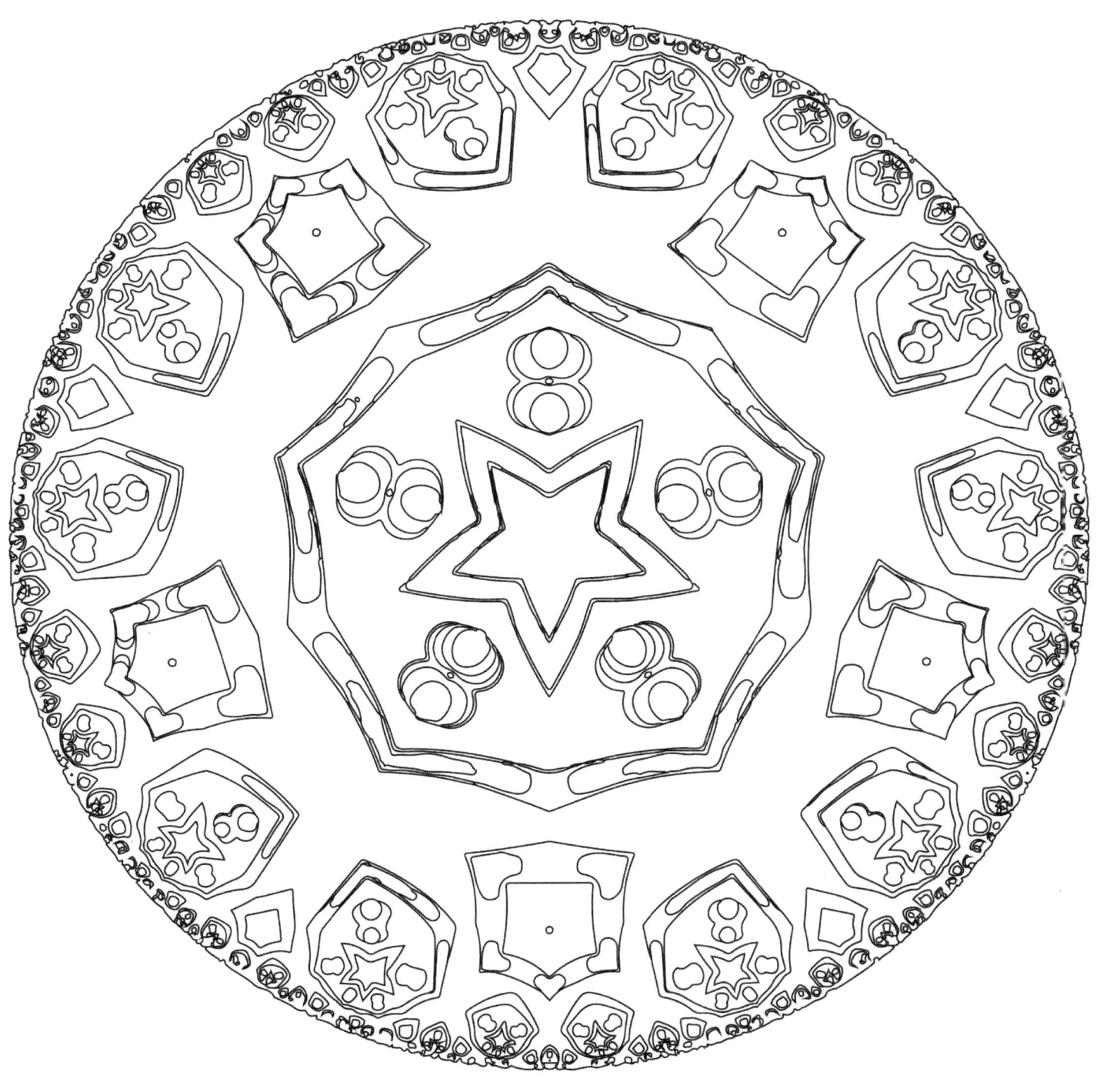

Activity 71: Circlesquare

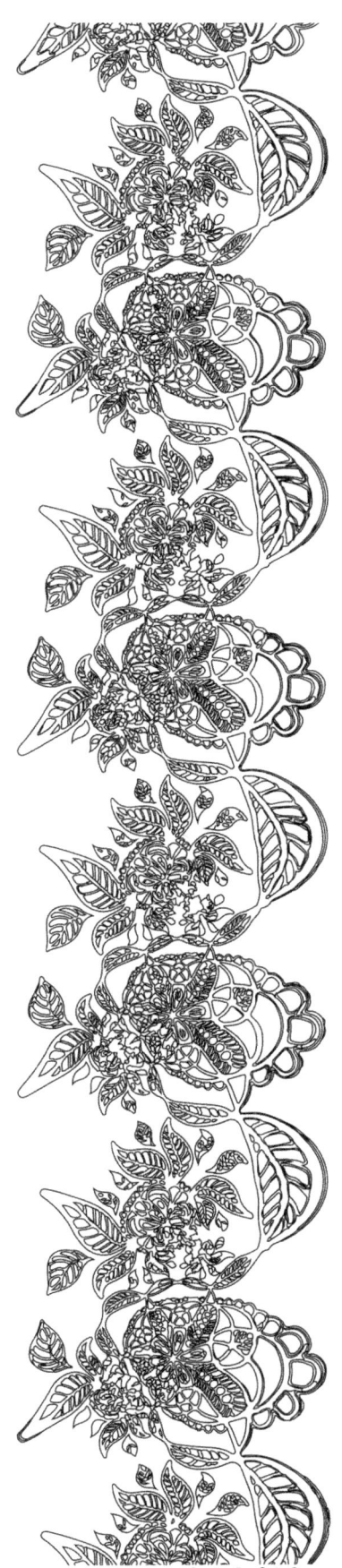

Activity 72: Milk & Cookies

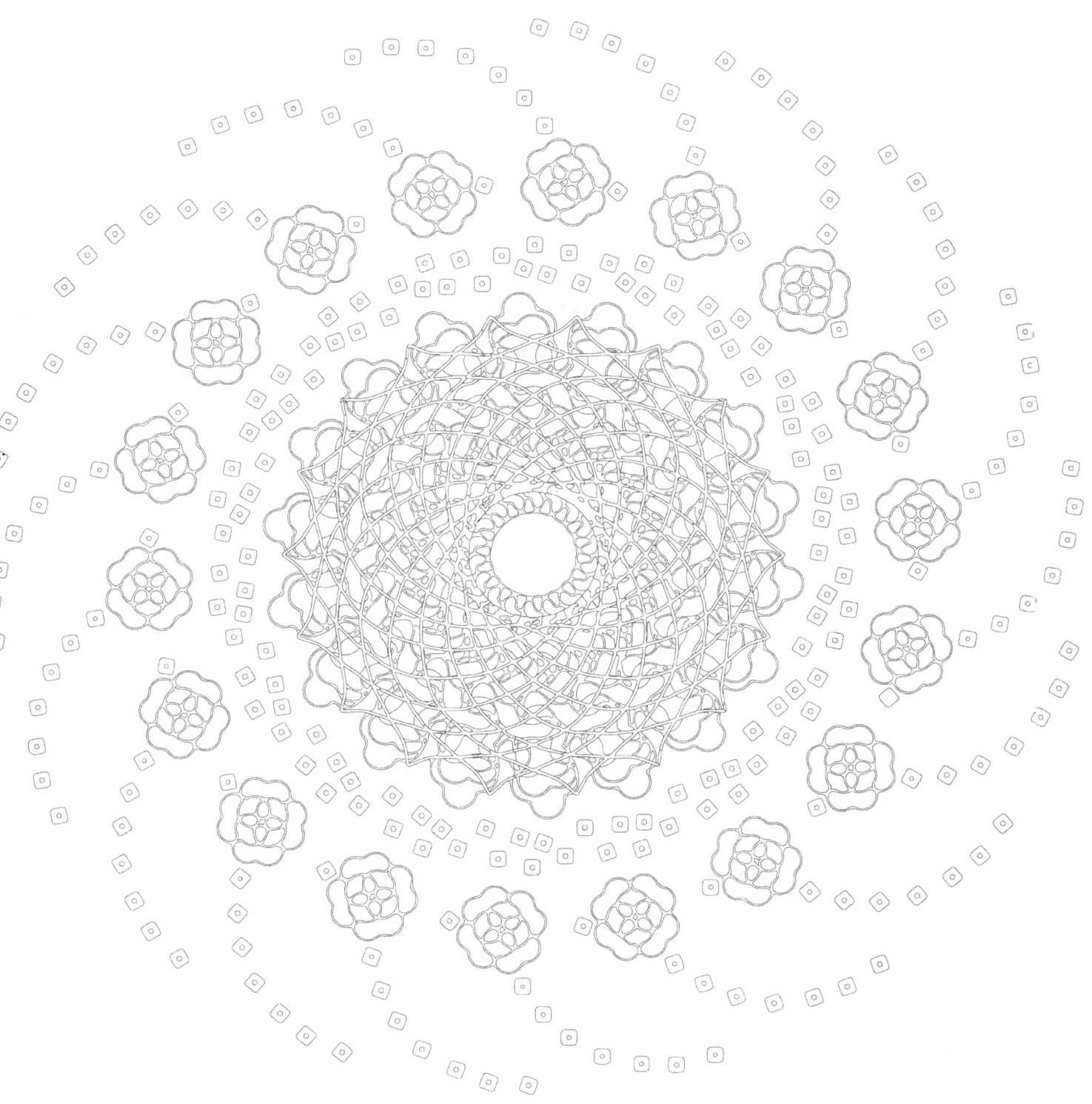

Activity 73: Golden rule

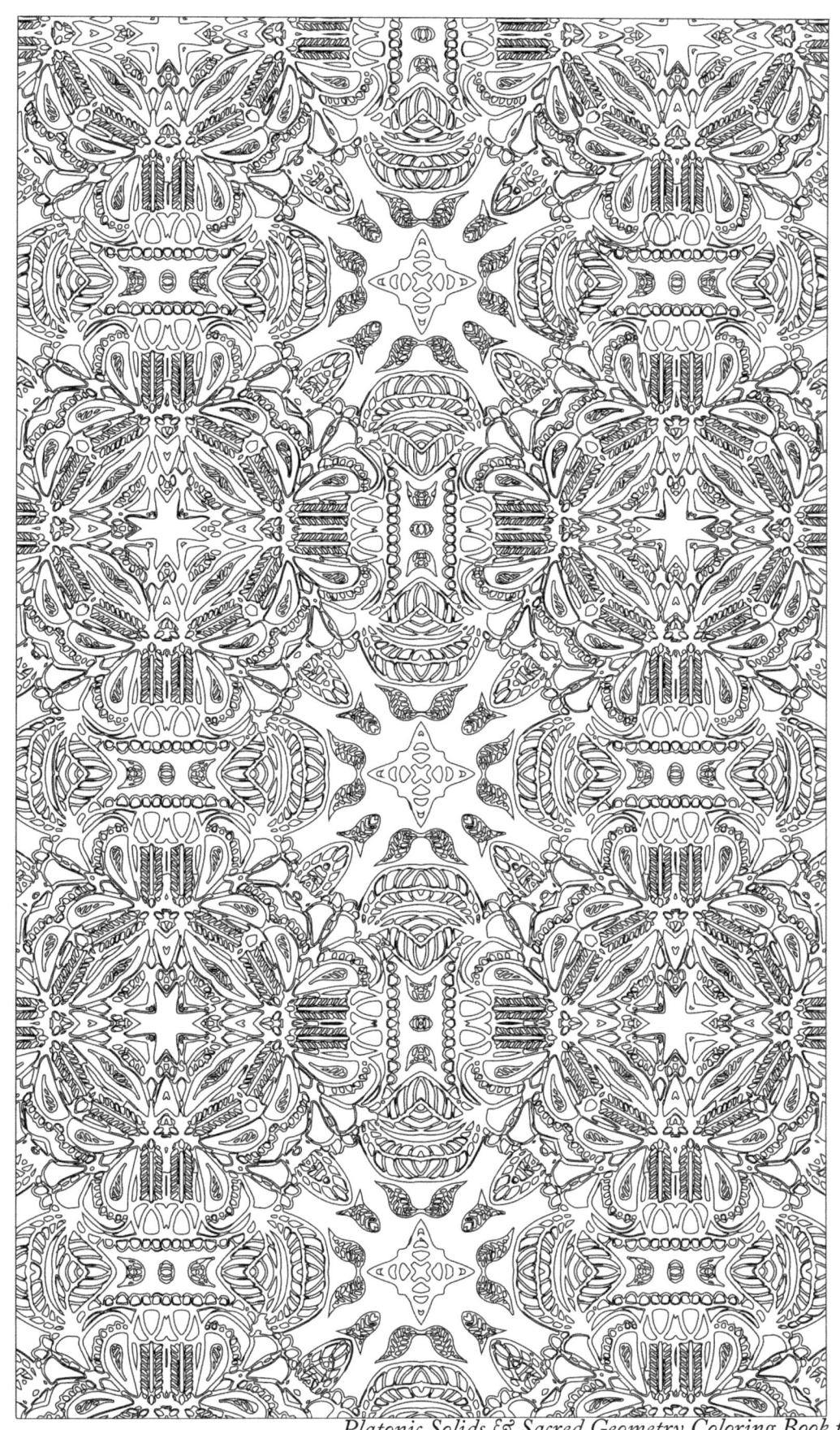

Activity 74: Continuity

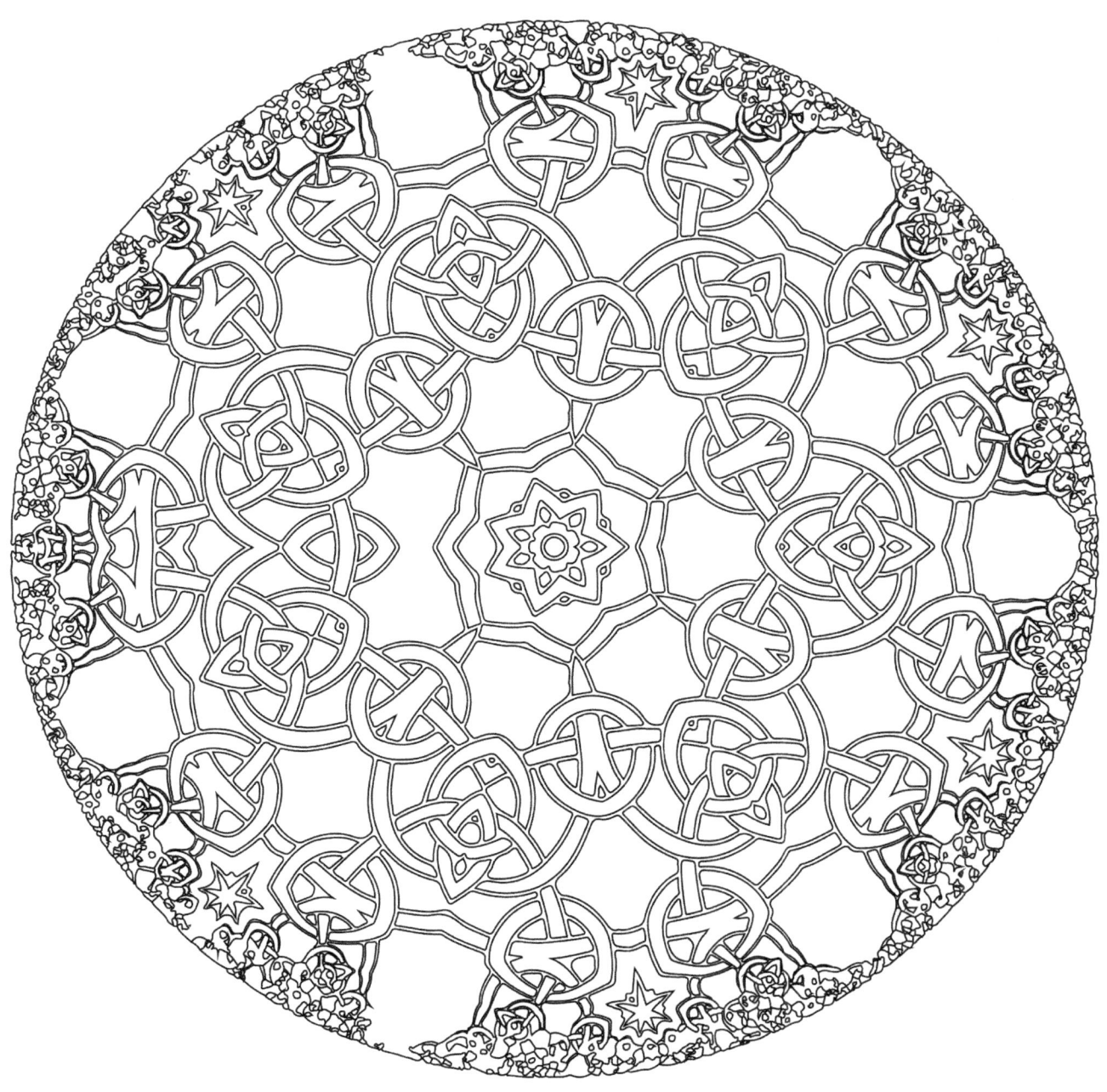

Activity 75: Connections

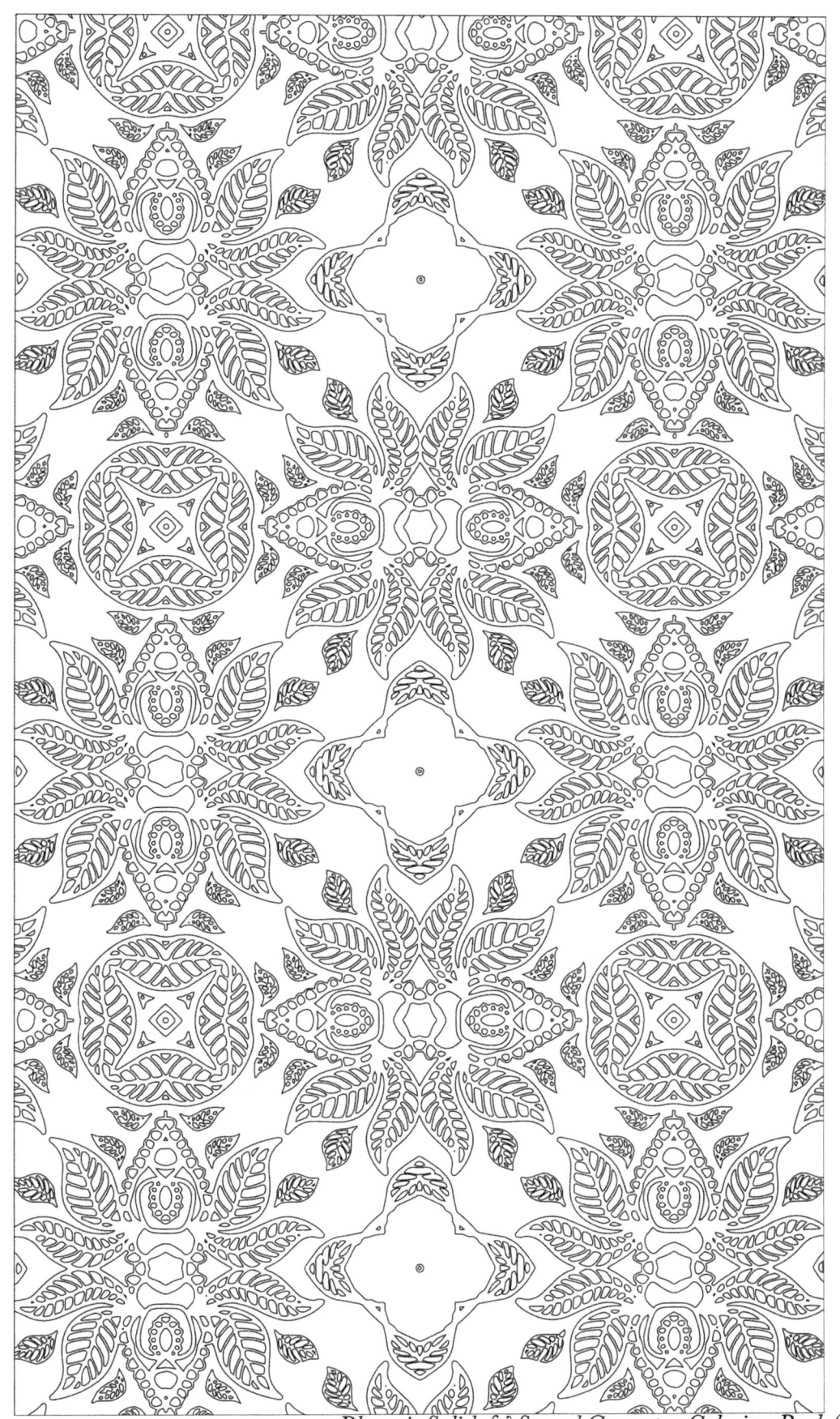

Activity 76: Two lovers

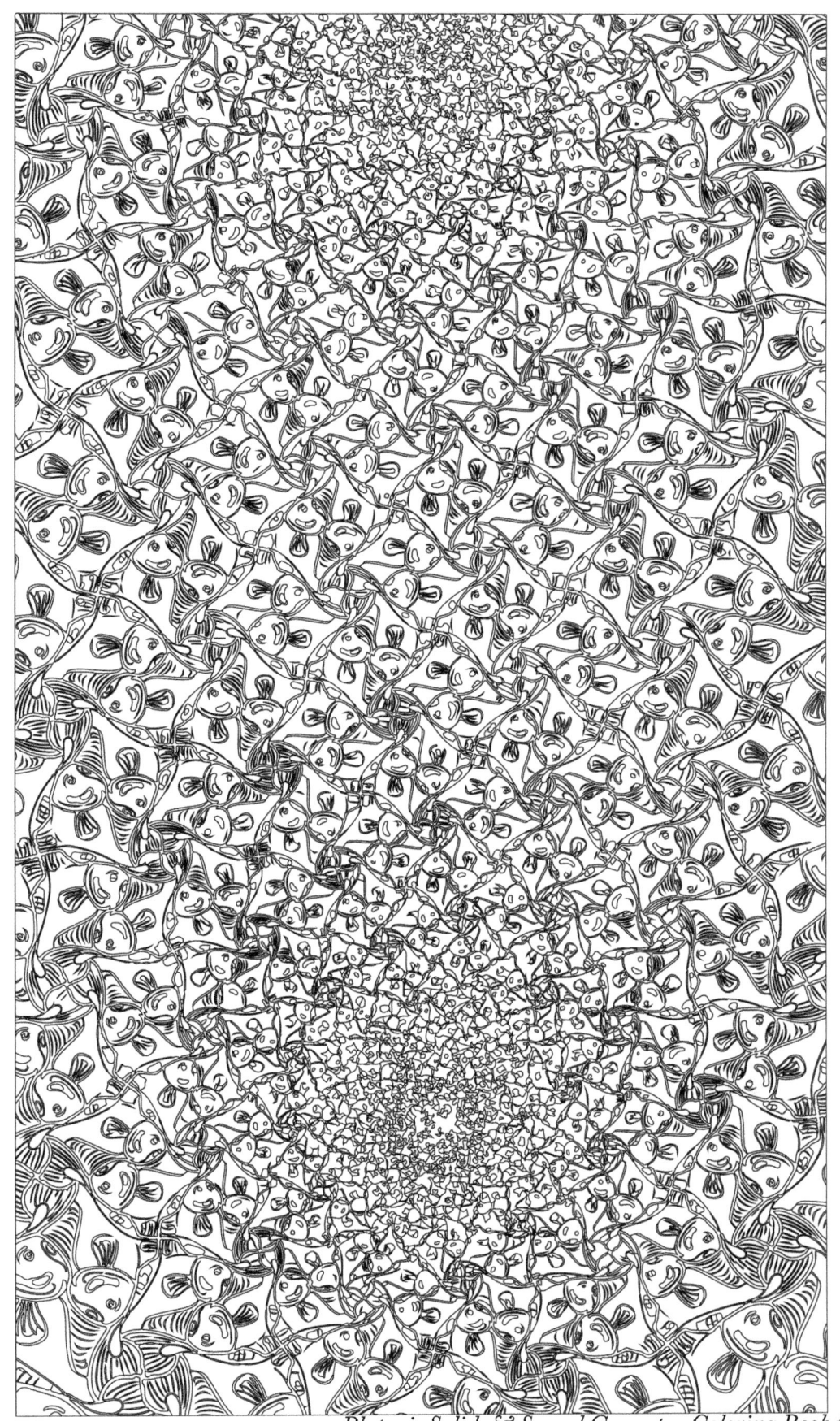

Platonic Solids & Sacred Geometry Coloring Book for Adults

Activity 77: Ice crystals

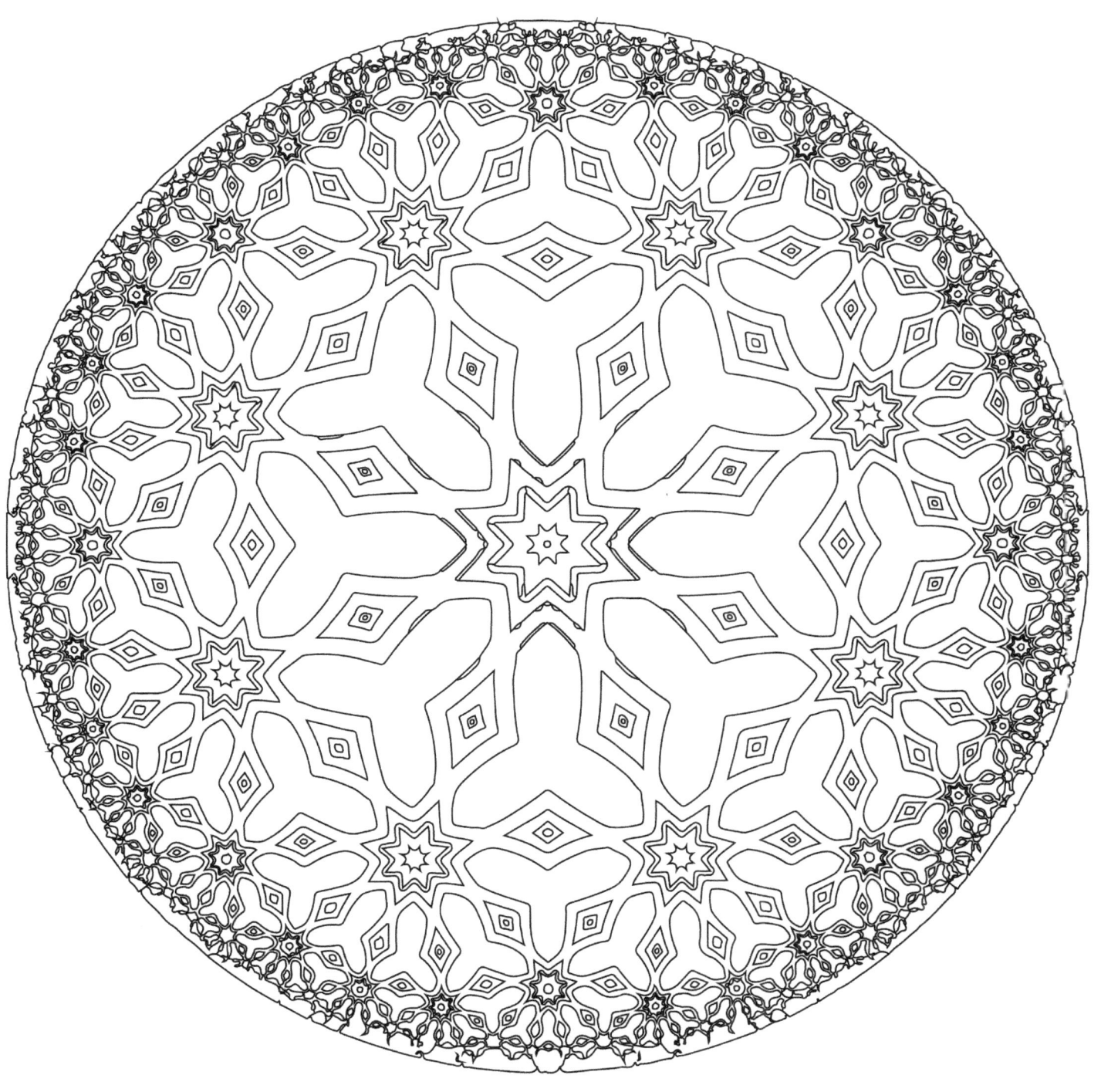

Activity 78: Point of no return

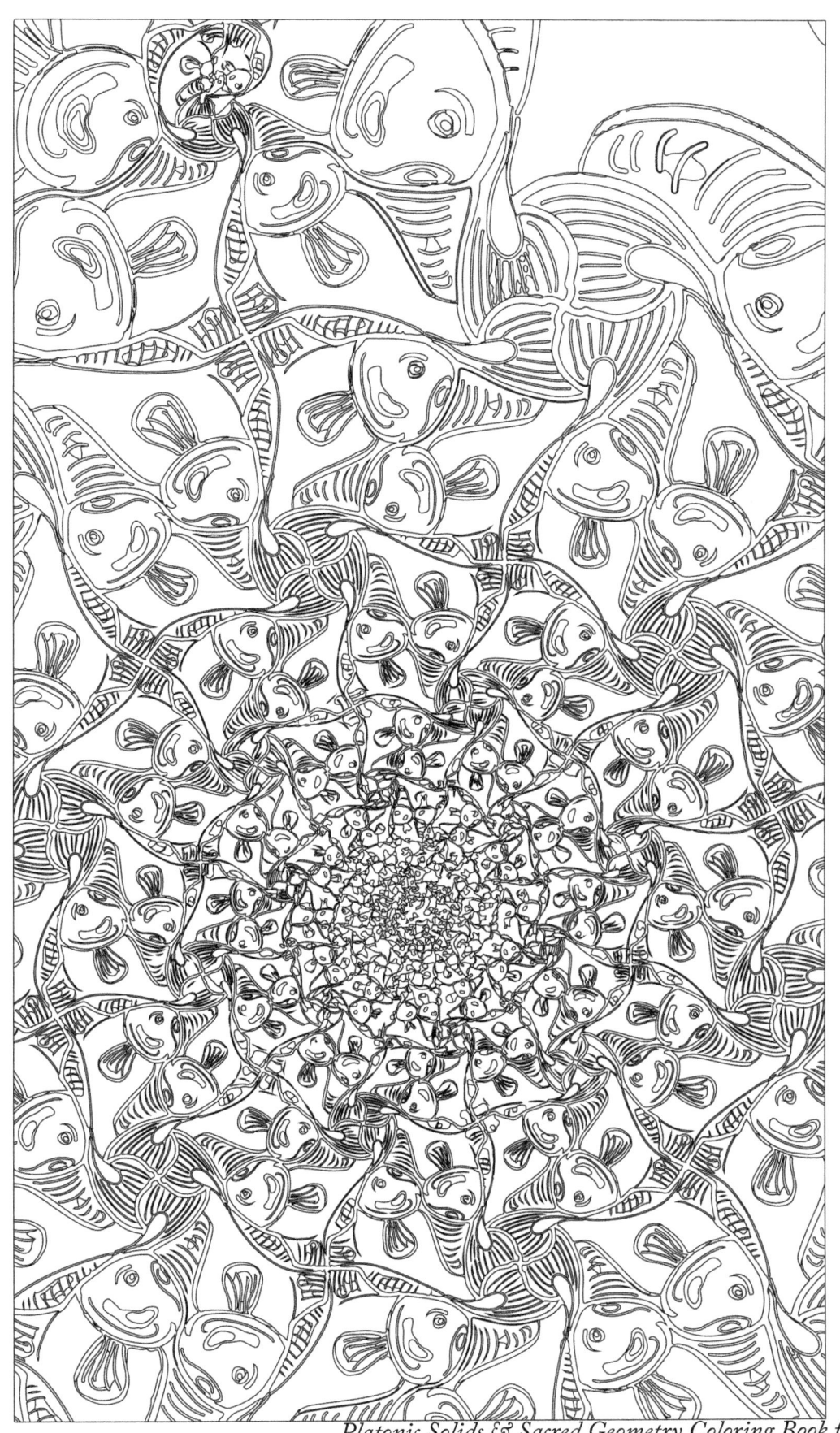

Activity 79: Fountain

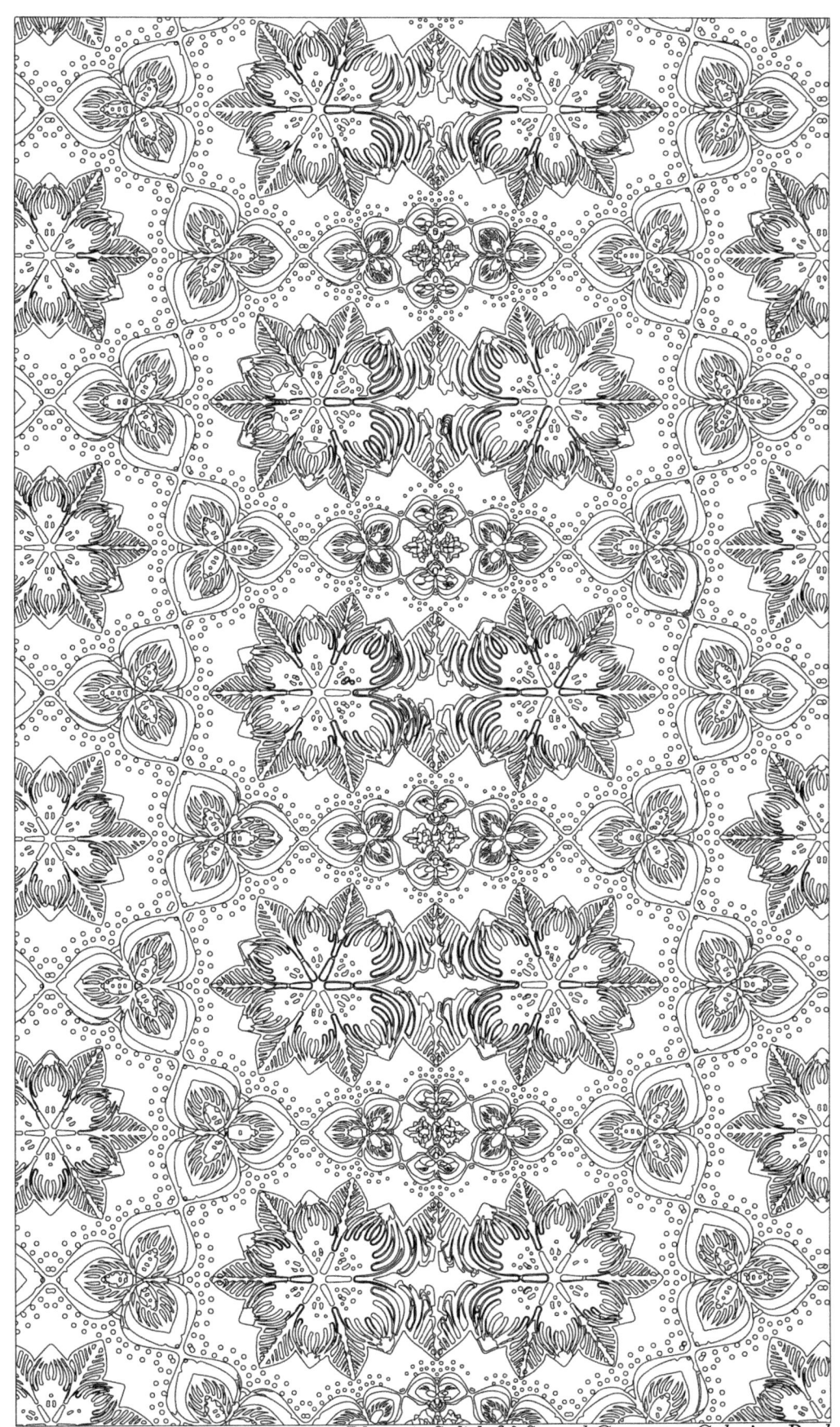

Activity 80: Patience

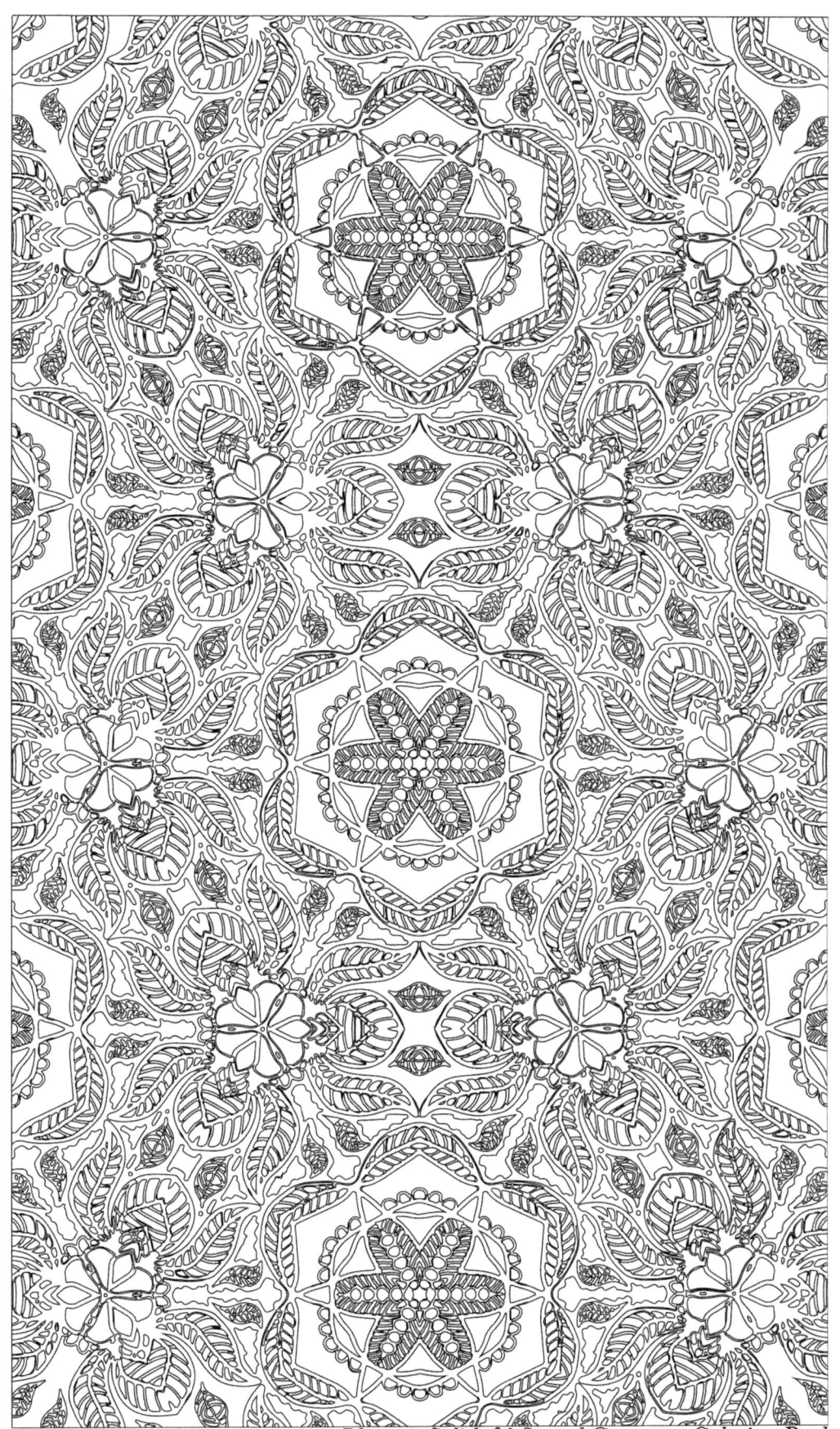

Activity 81: Imperfect triangle

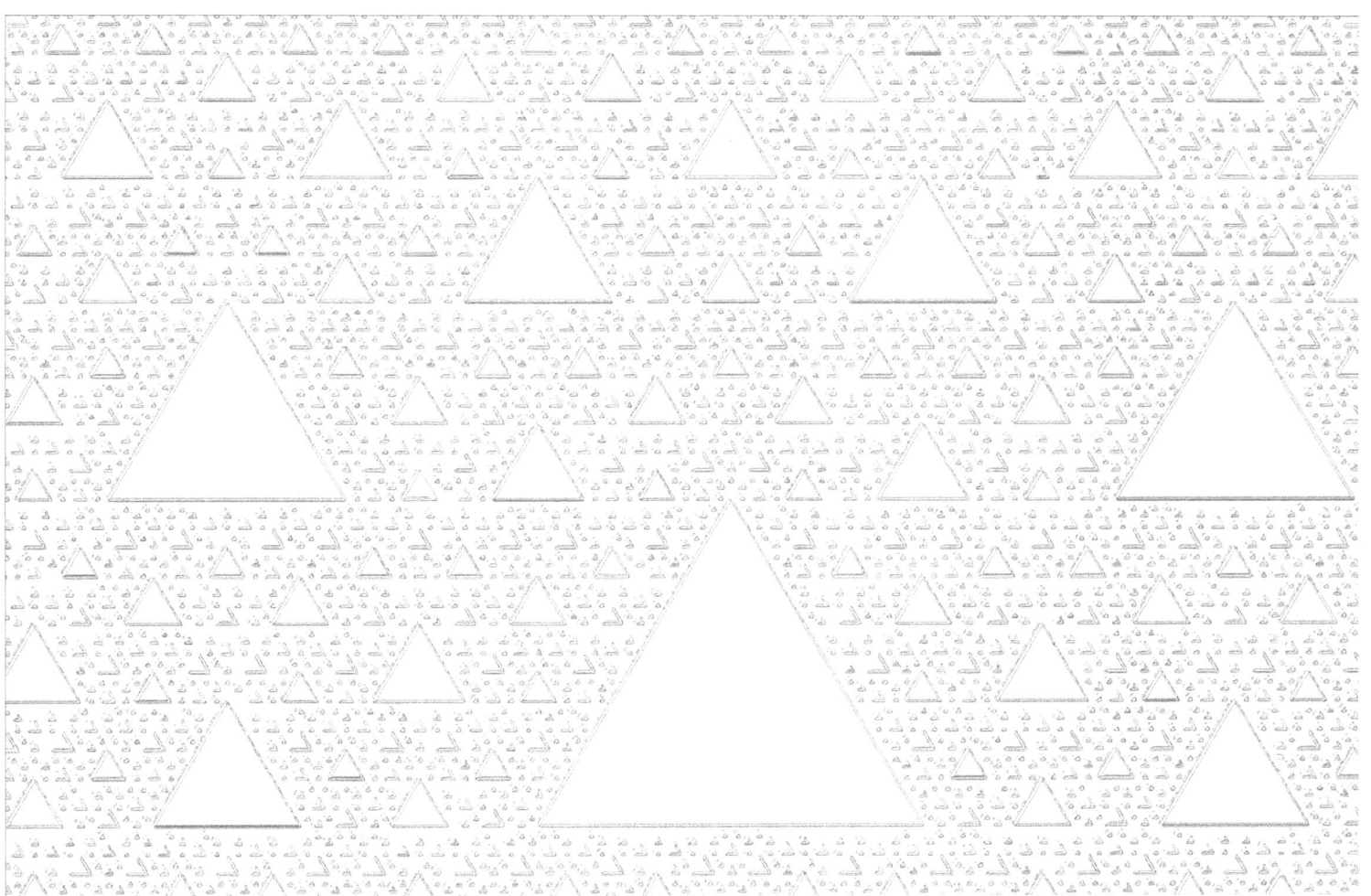

Activity 82: God

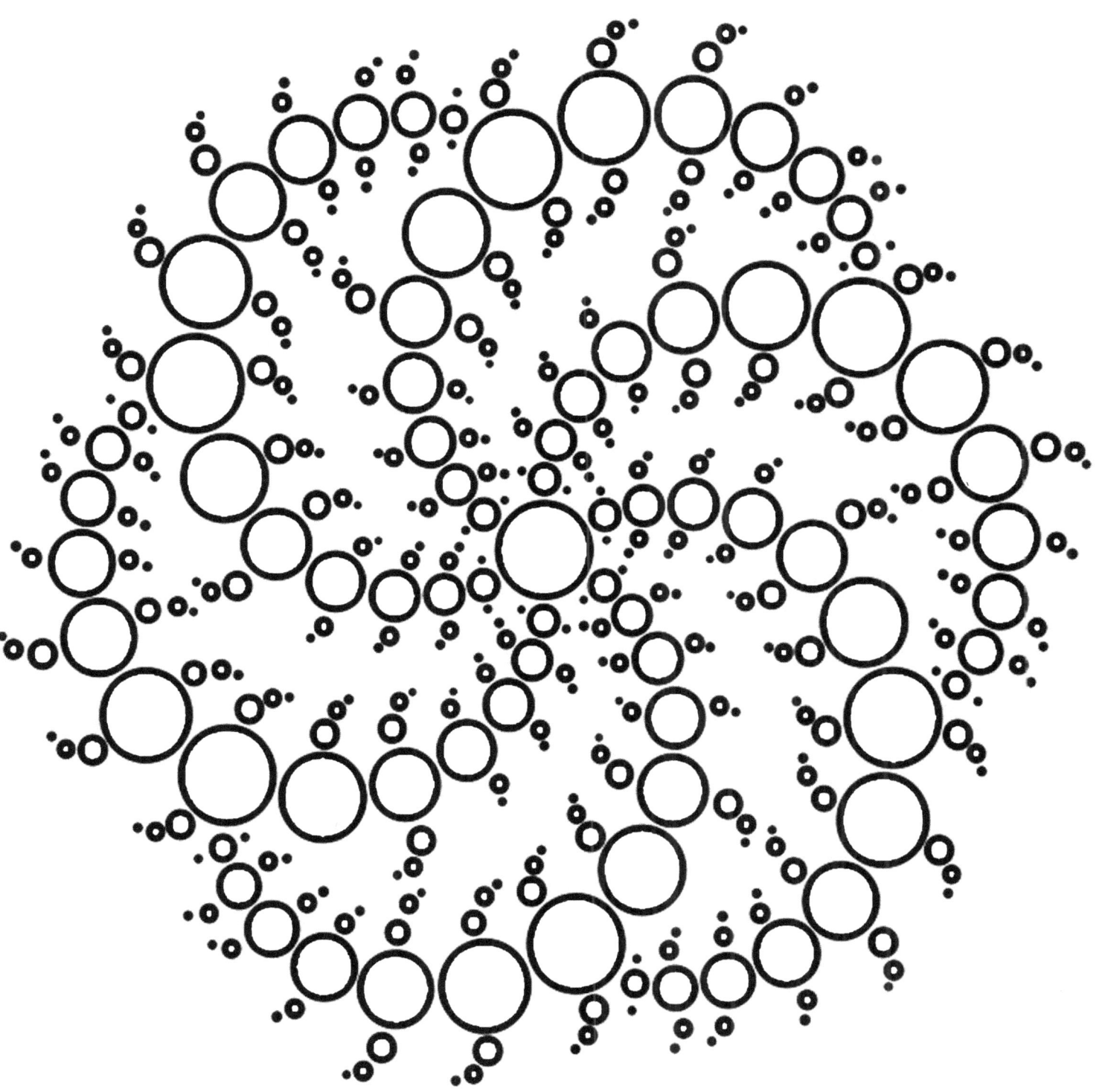

Platonic Solids & Sacred Geometry Coloring Book for Adults

Activity 83: Pond

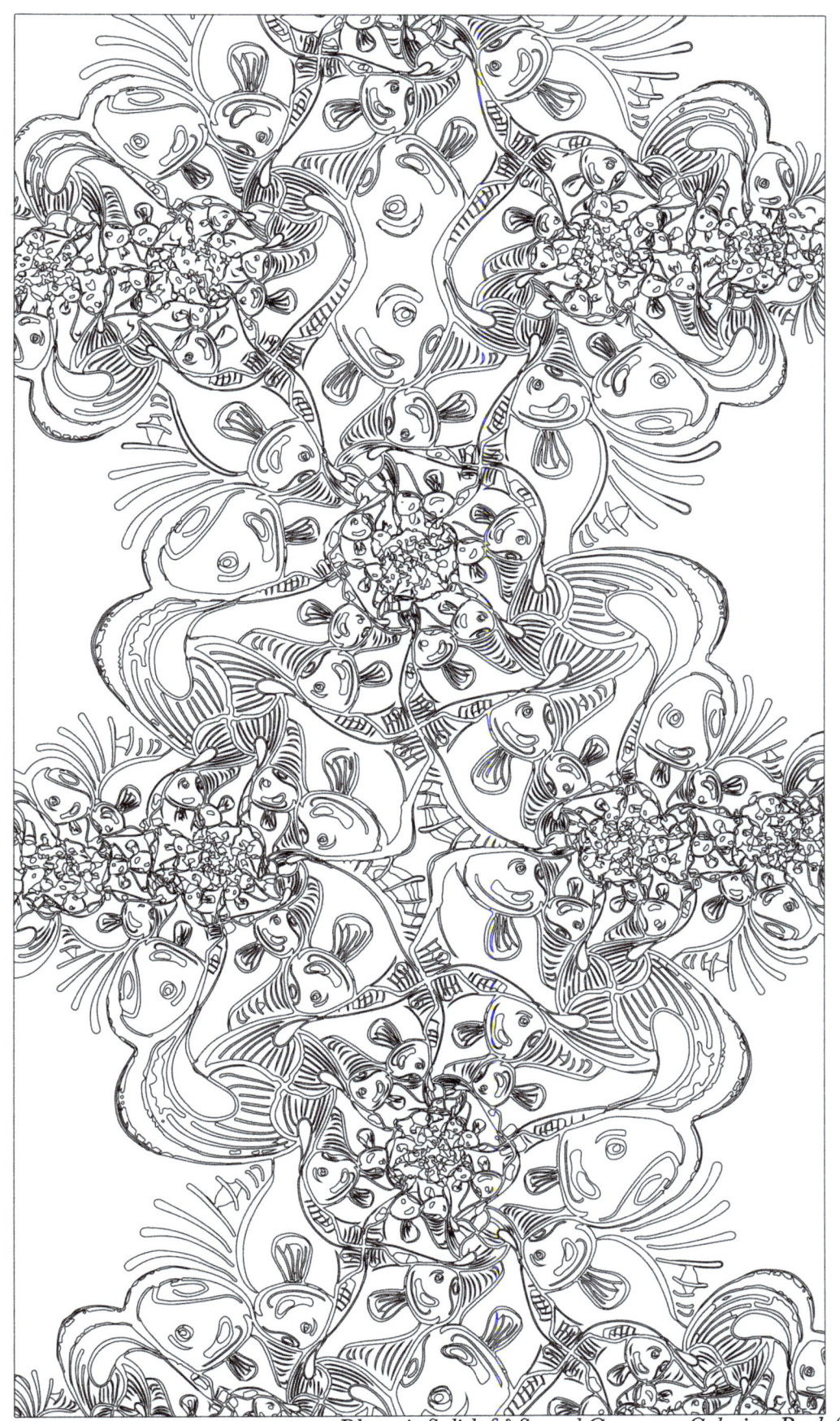

Activity 84: Electrotechnical

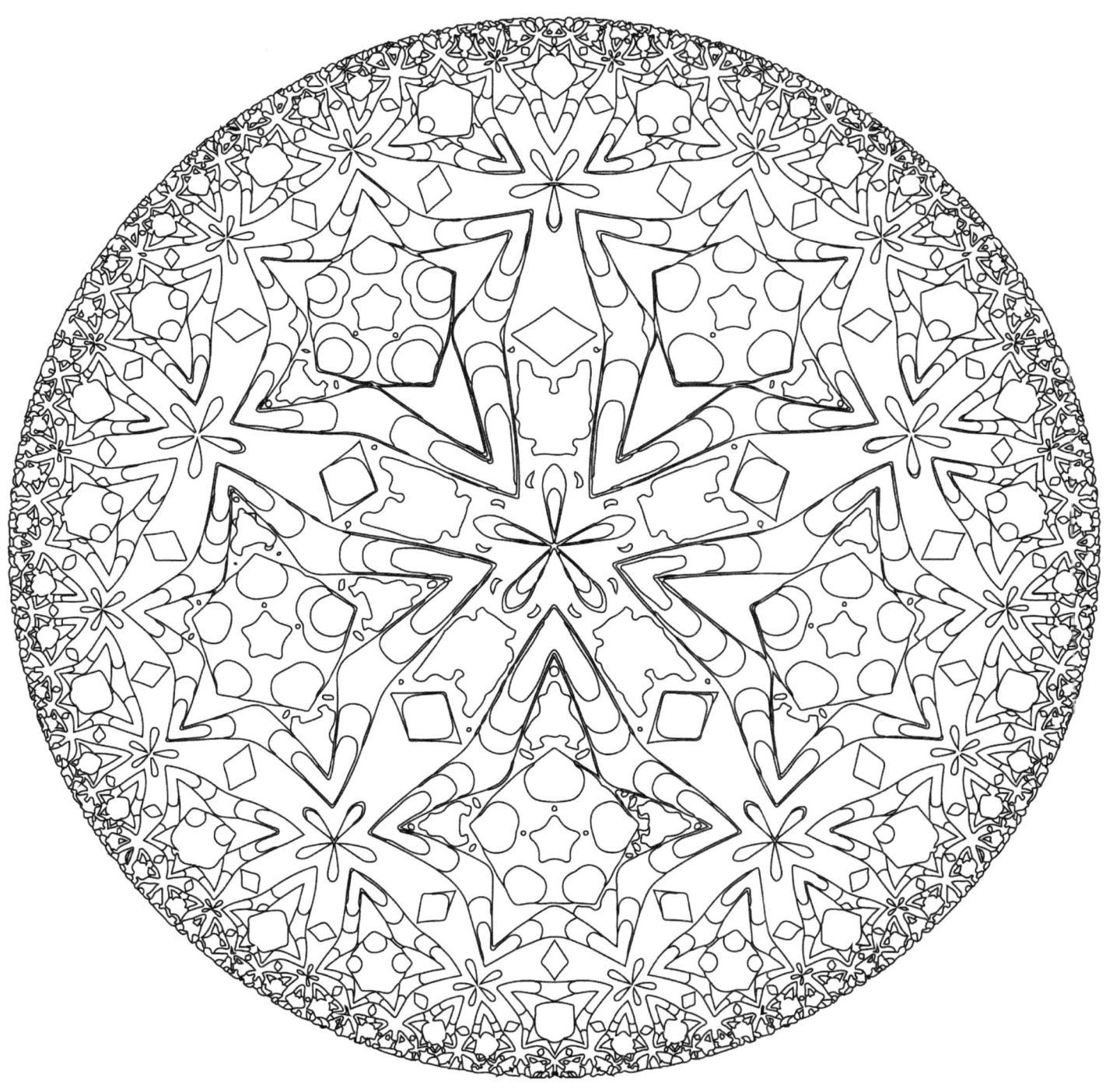

Activity 85: Star circumference

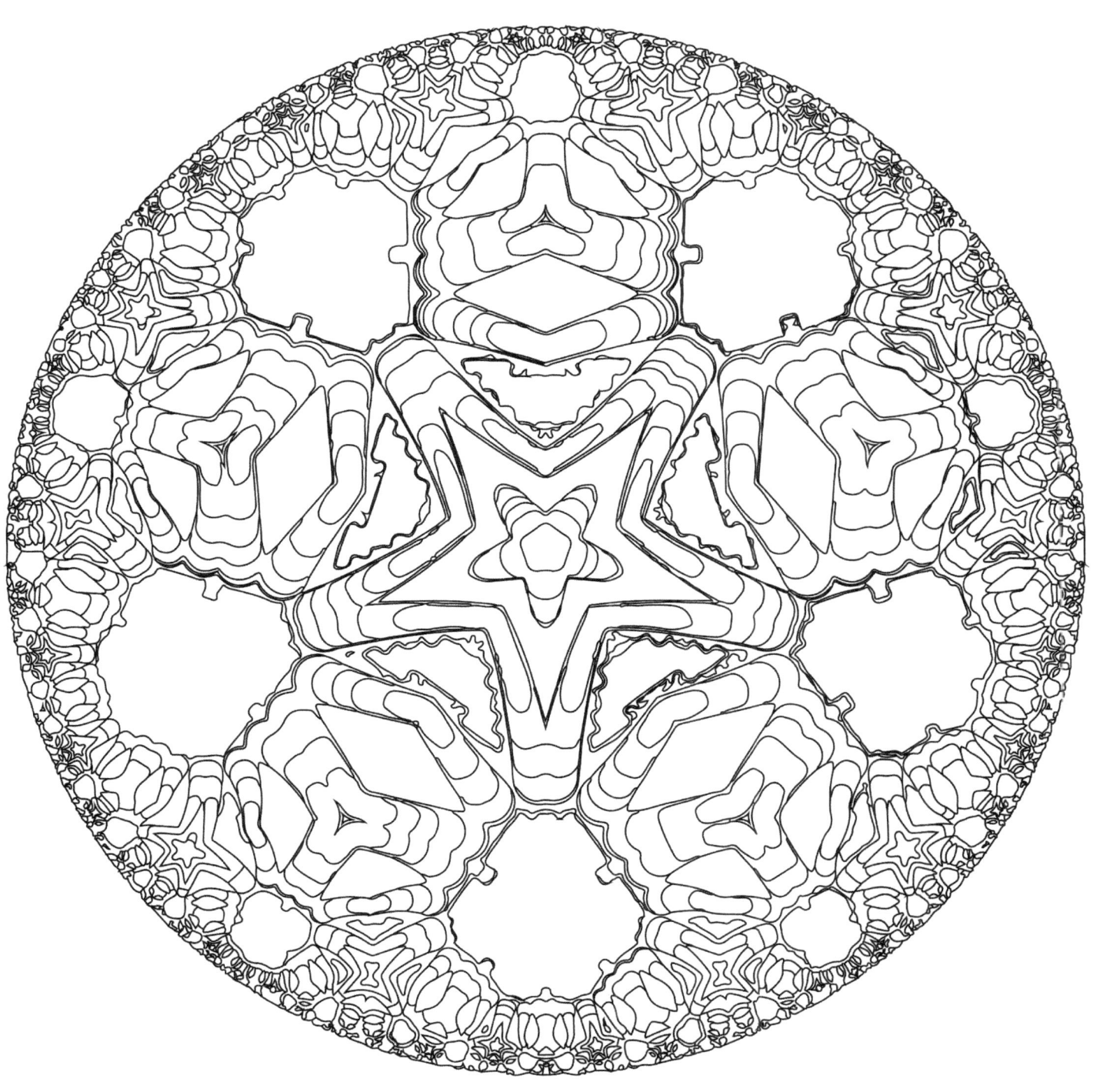

Activity 86: Holy of Holies

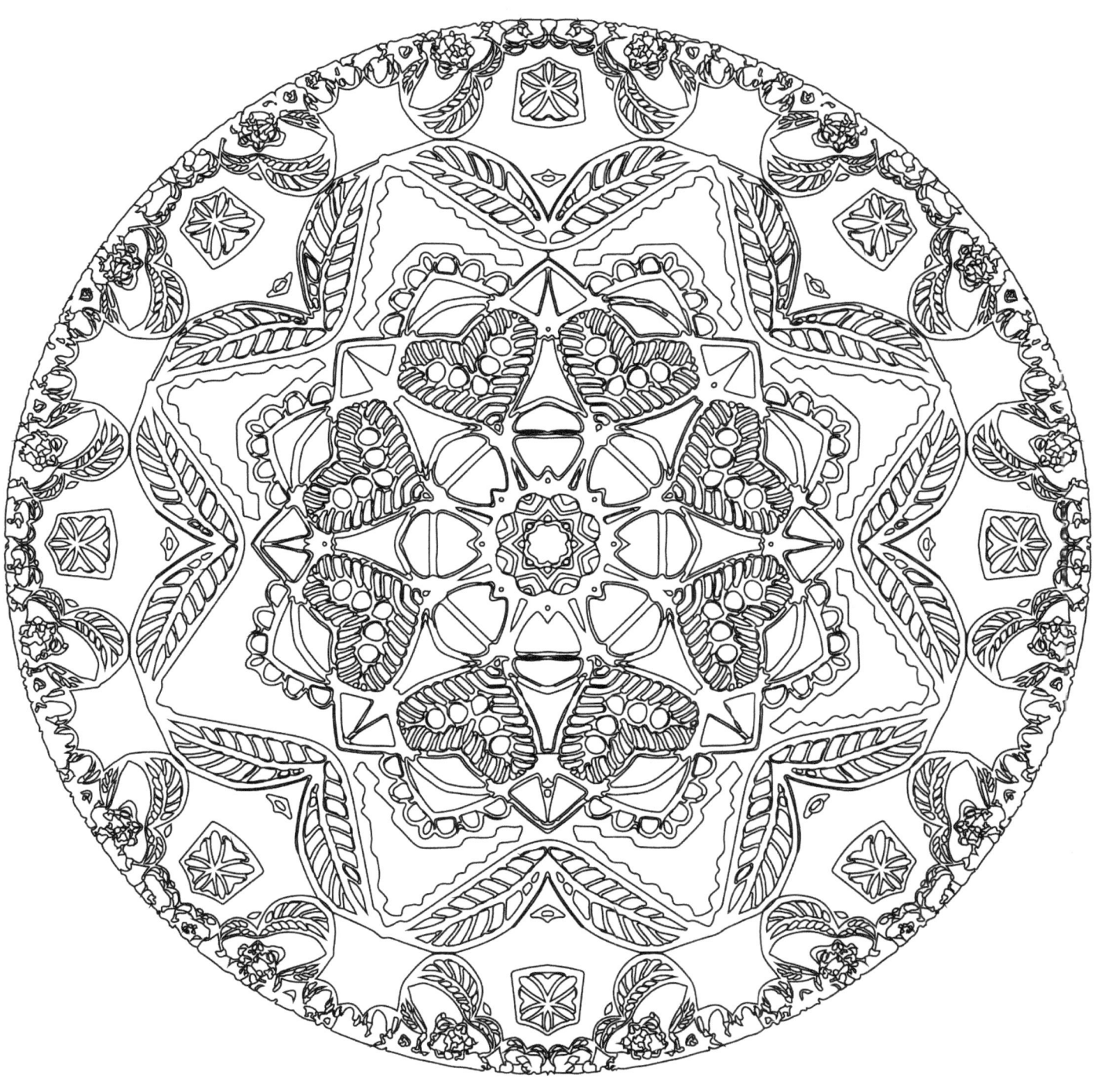

Activity 87: Atom of peace

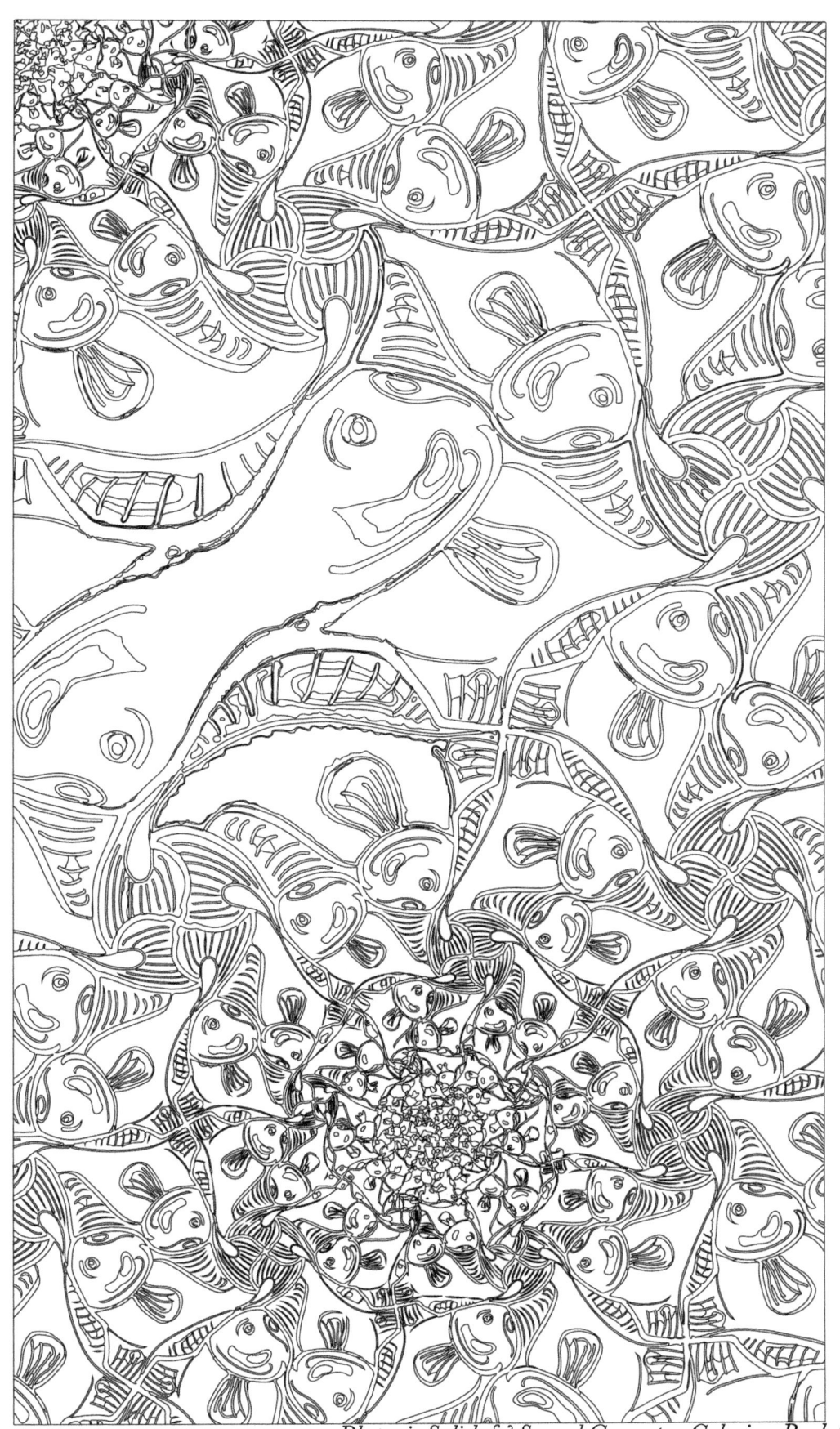

Activity 88: Roses of love

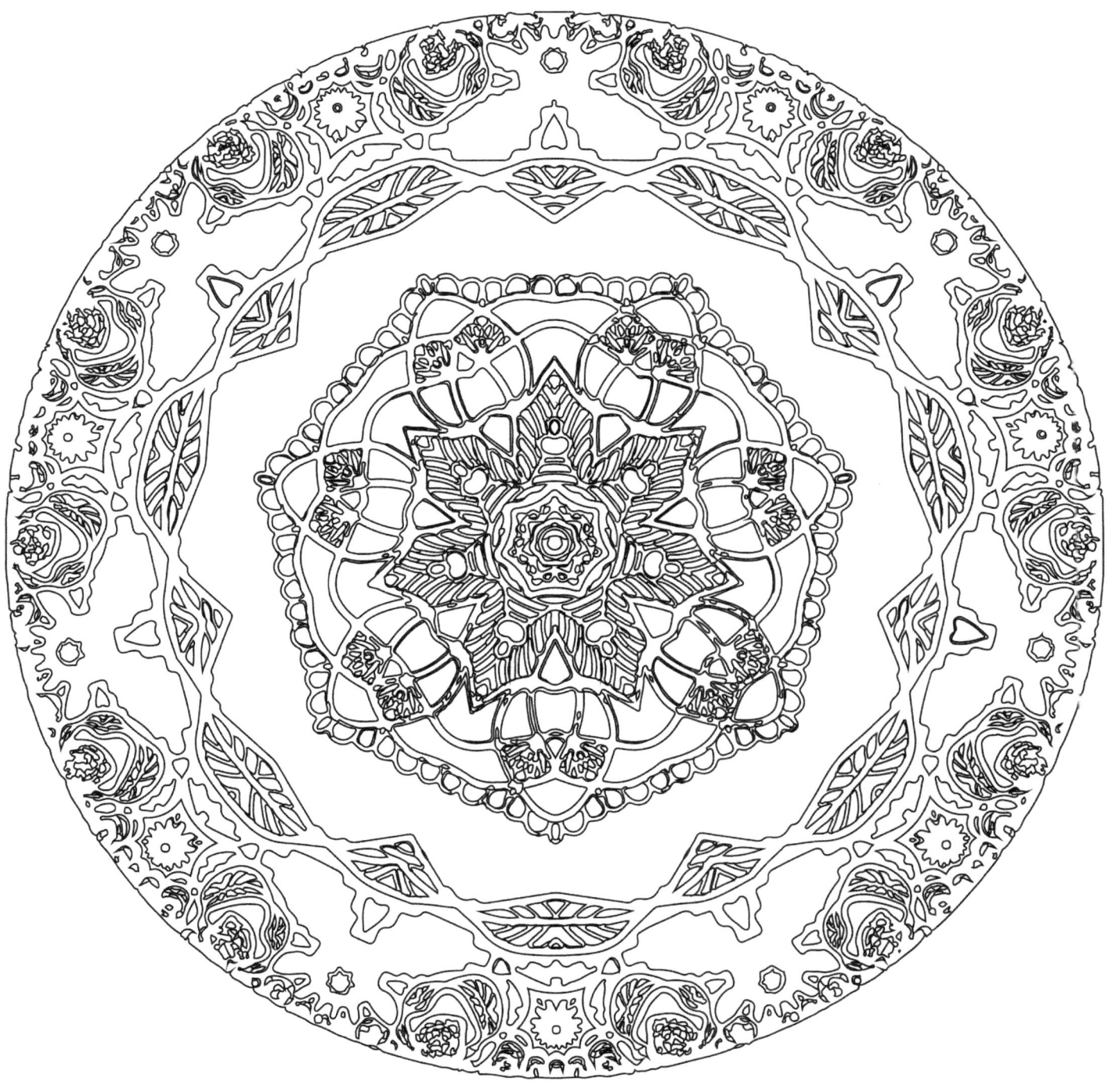

Platonic Solids & Sacred Geometry Coloring Book for Adults

Activity 89: Perfect beauty

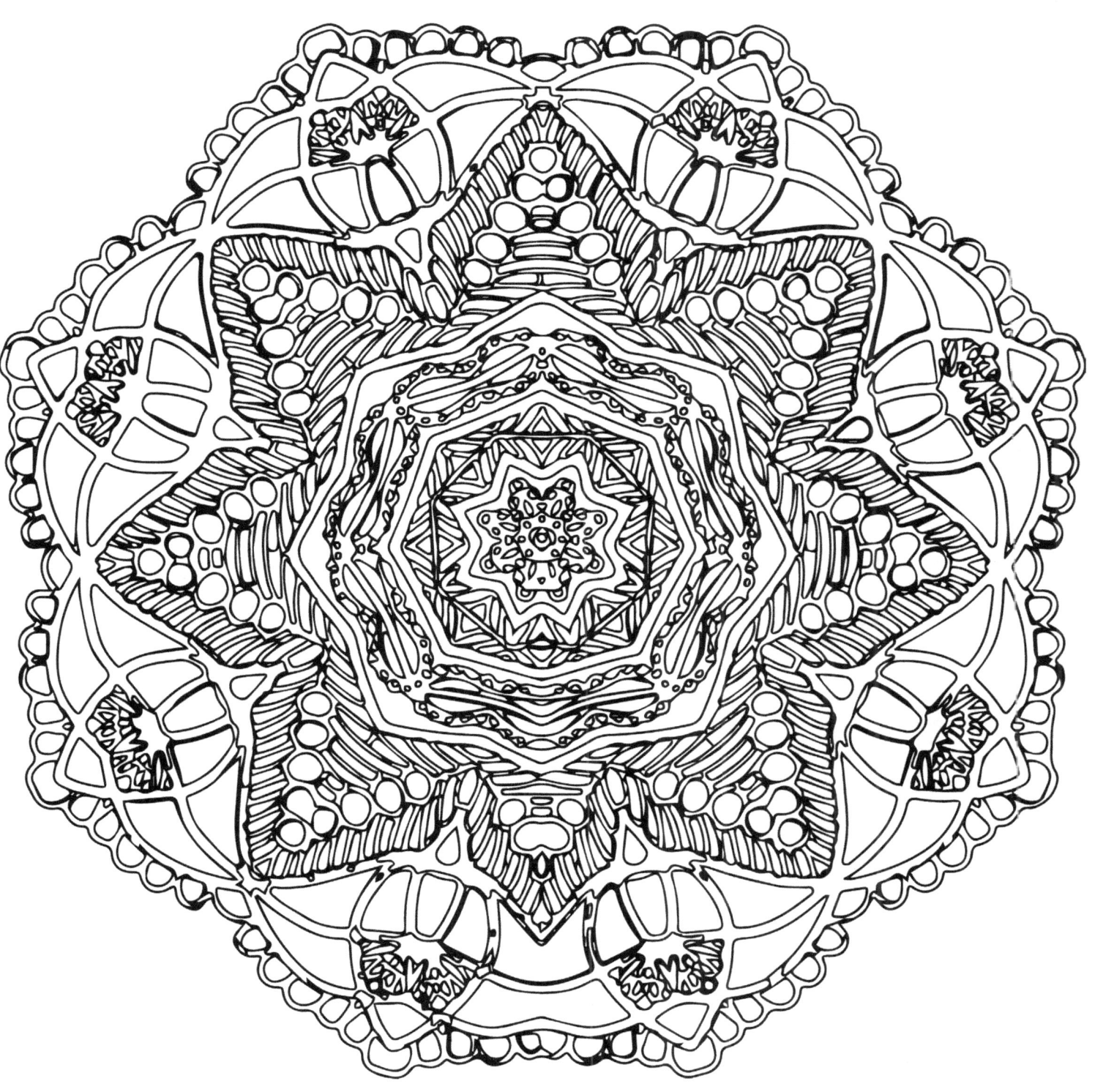

Activity 90: Endogendo

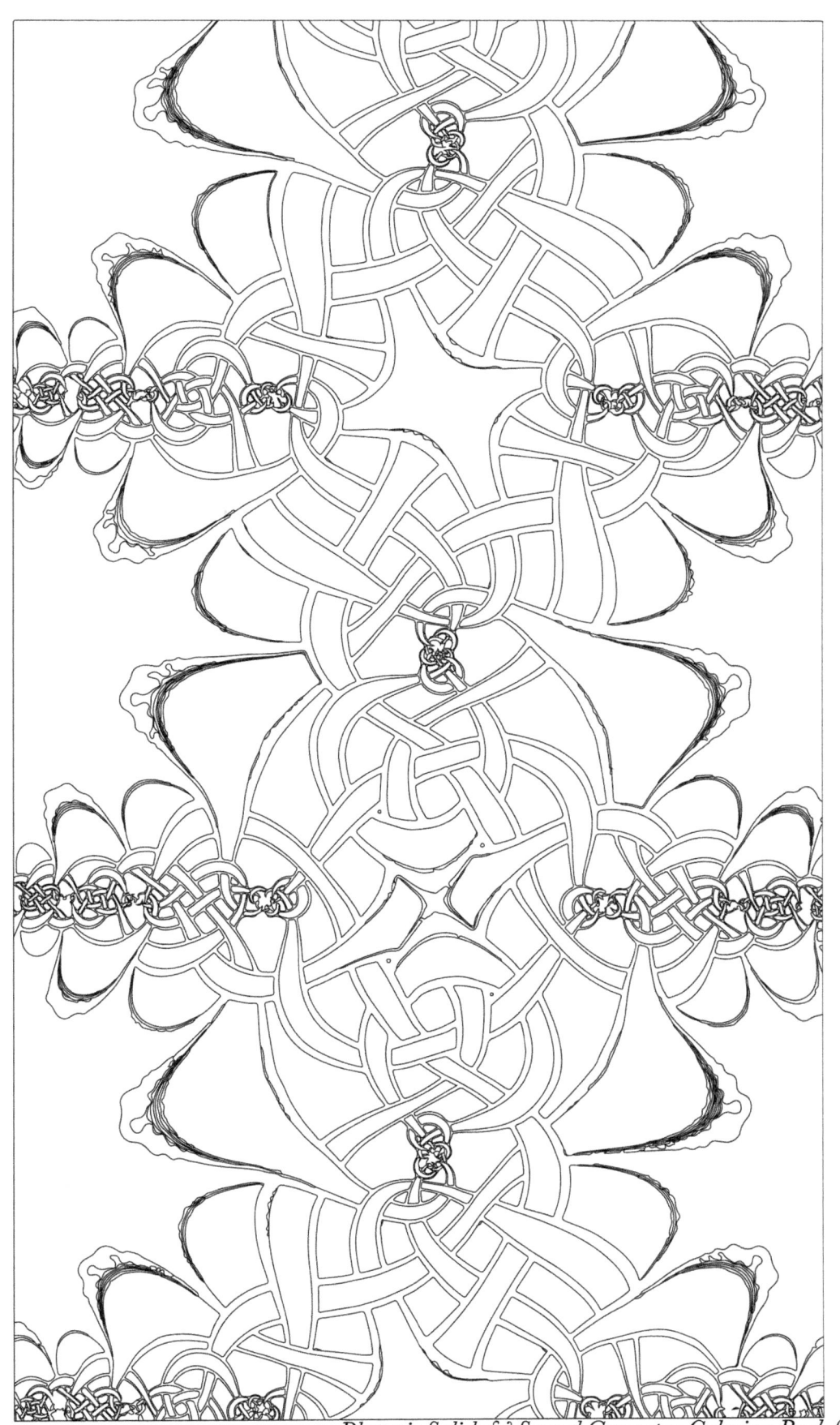

Activity 91: Melindano

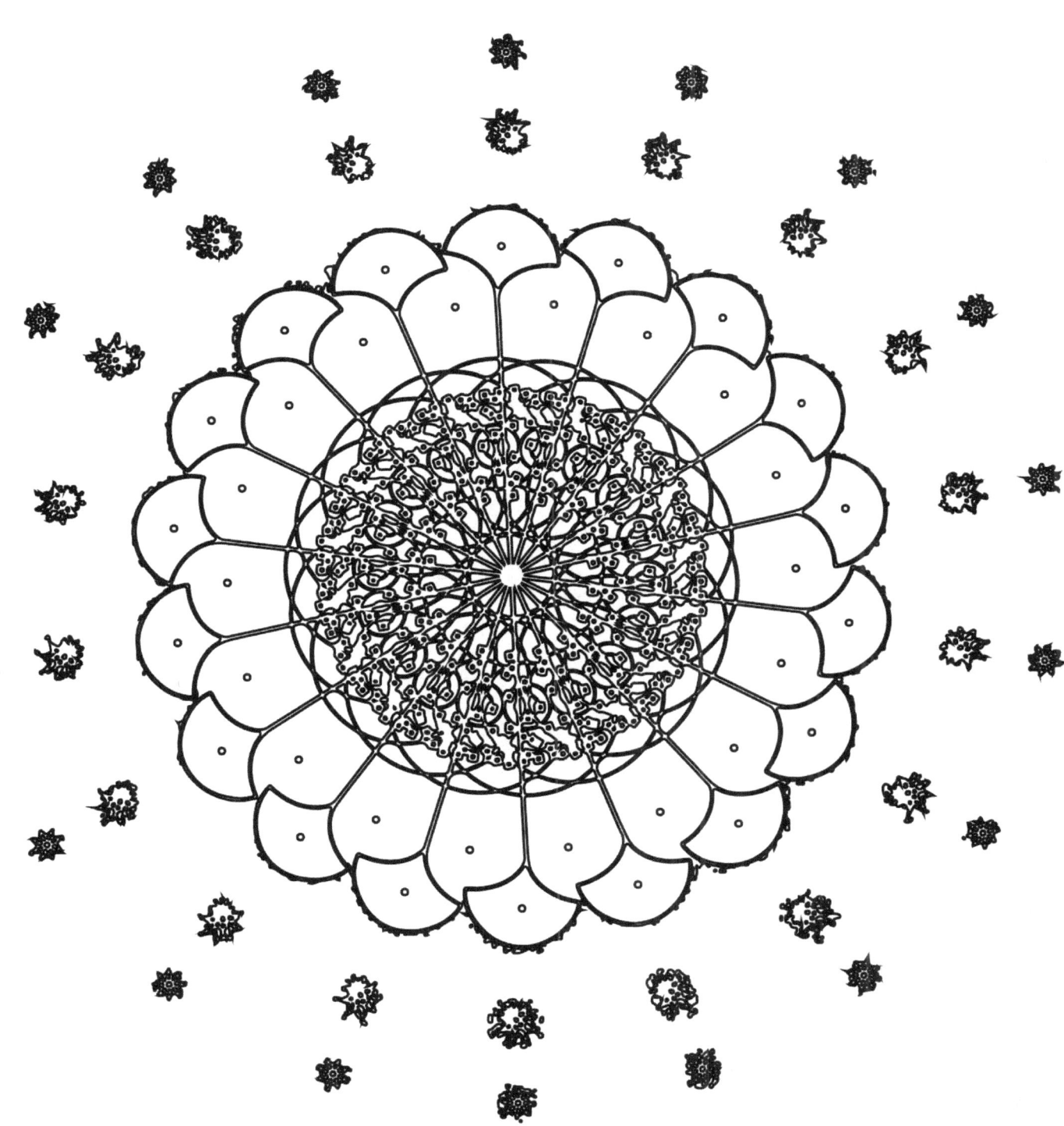

Activity 92: Hologram

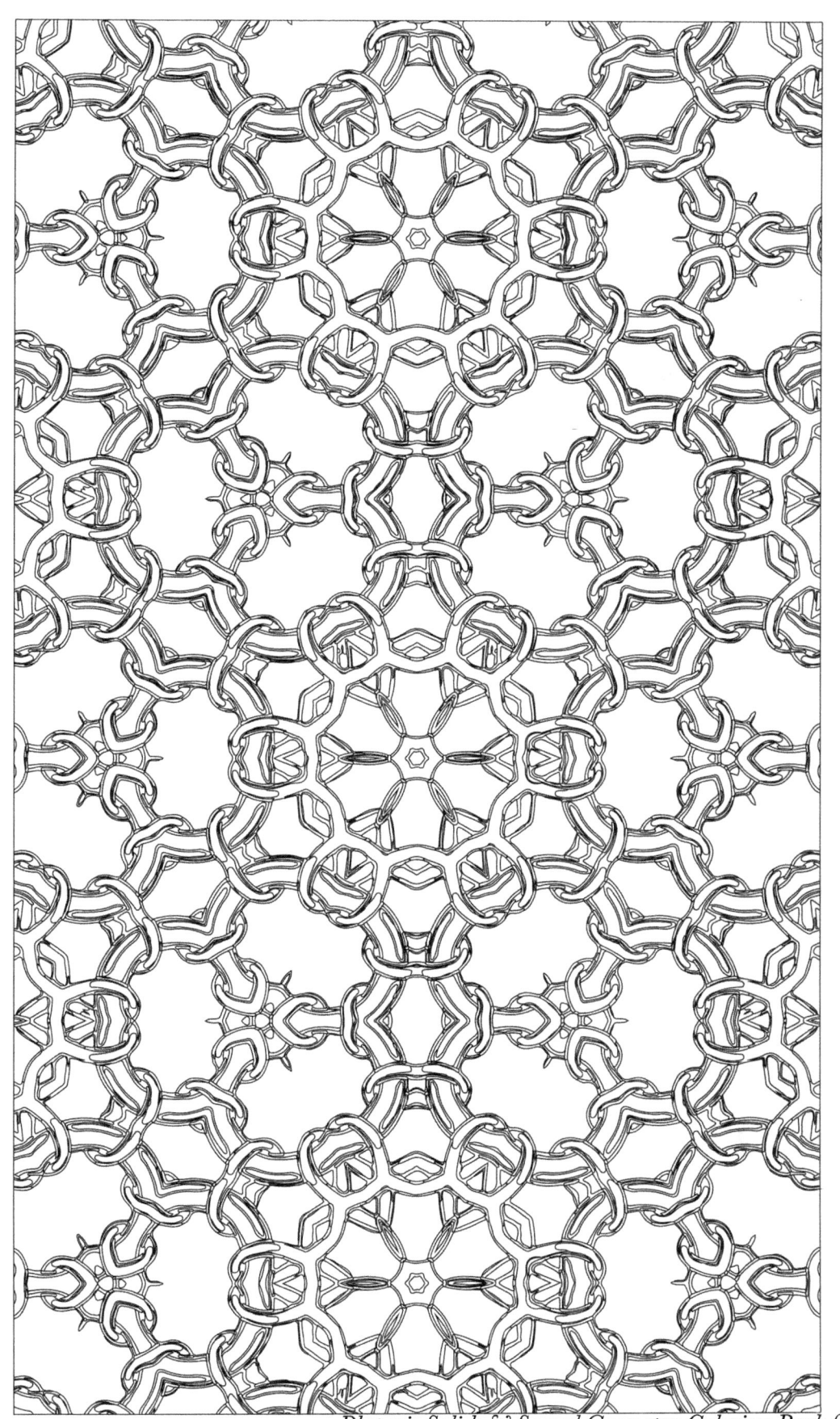

Activity 93: Multiverse theory

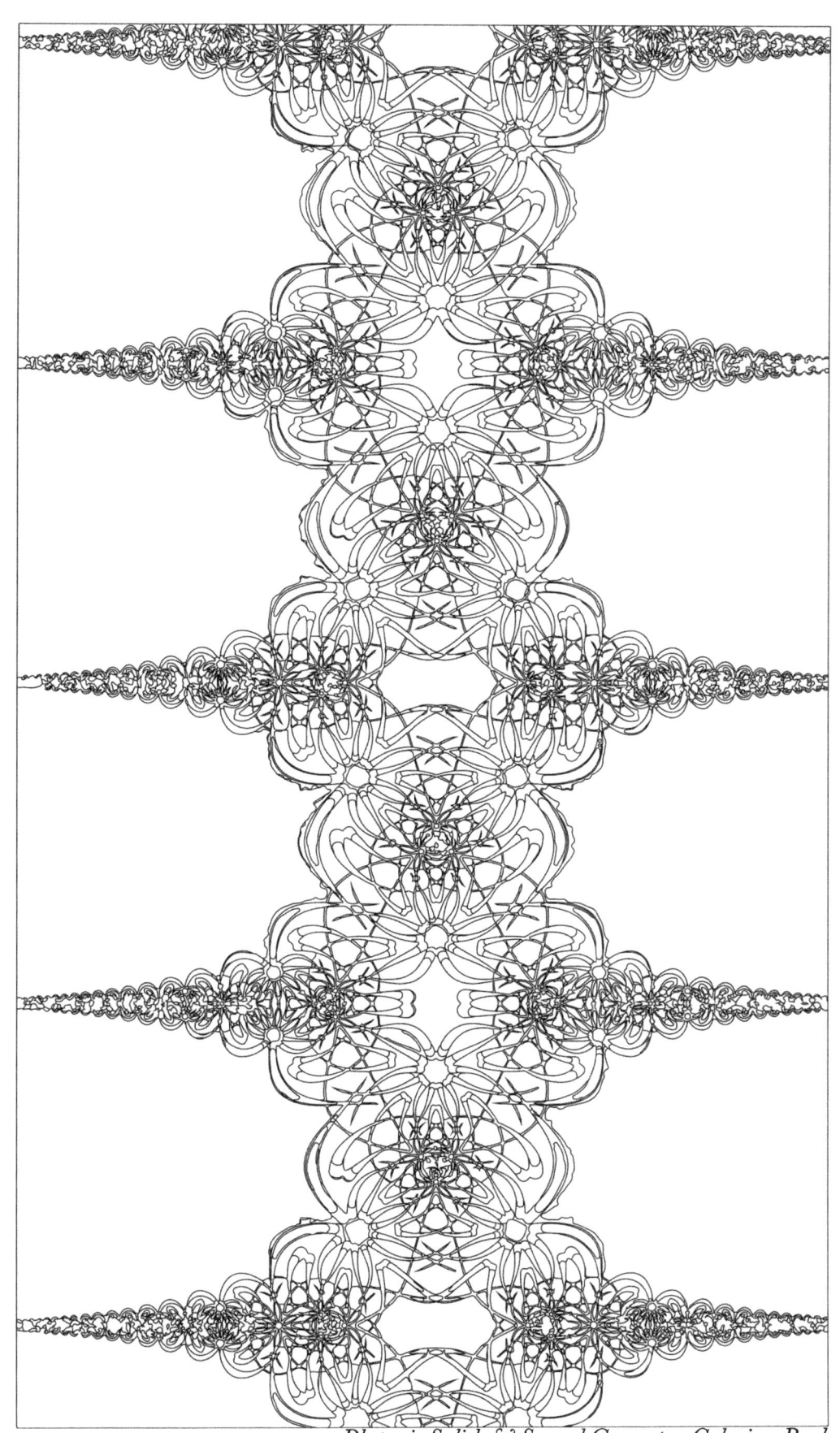

Activity 94: Seed multiplication

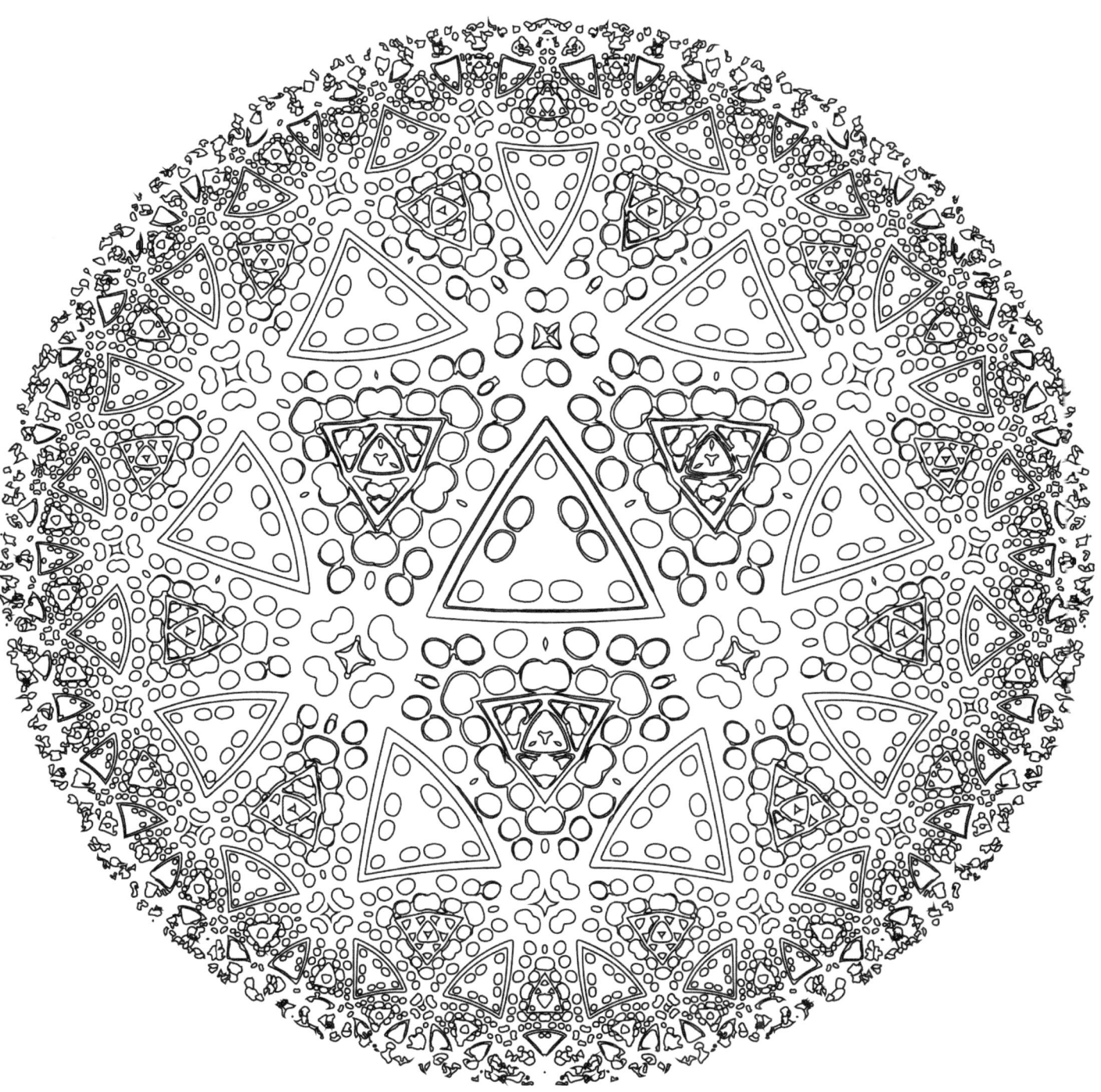

Activity 95: Square in circle

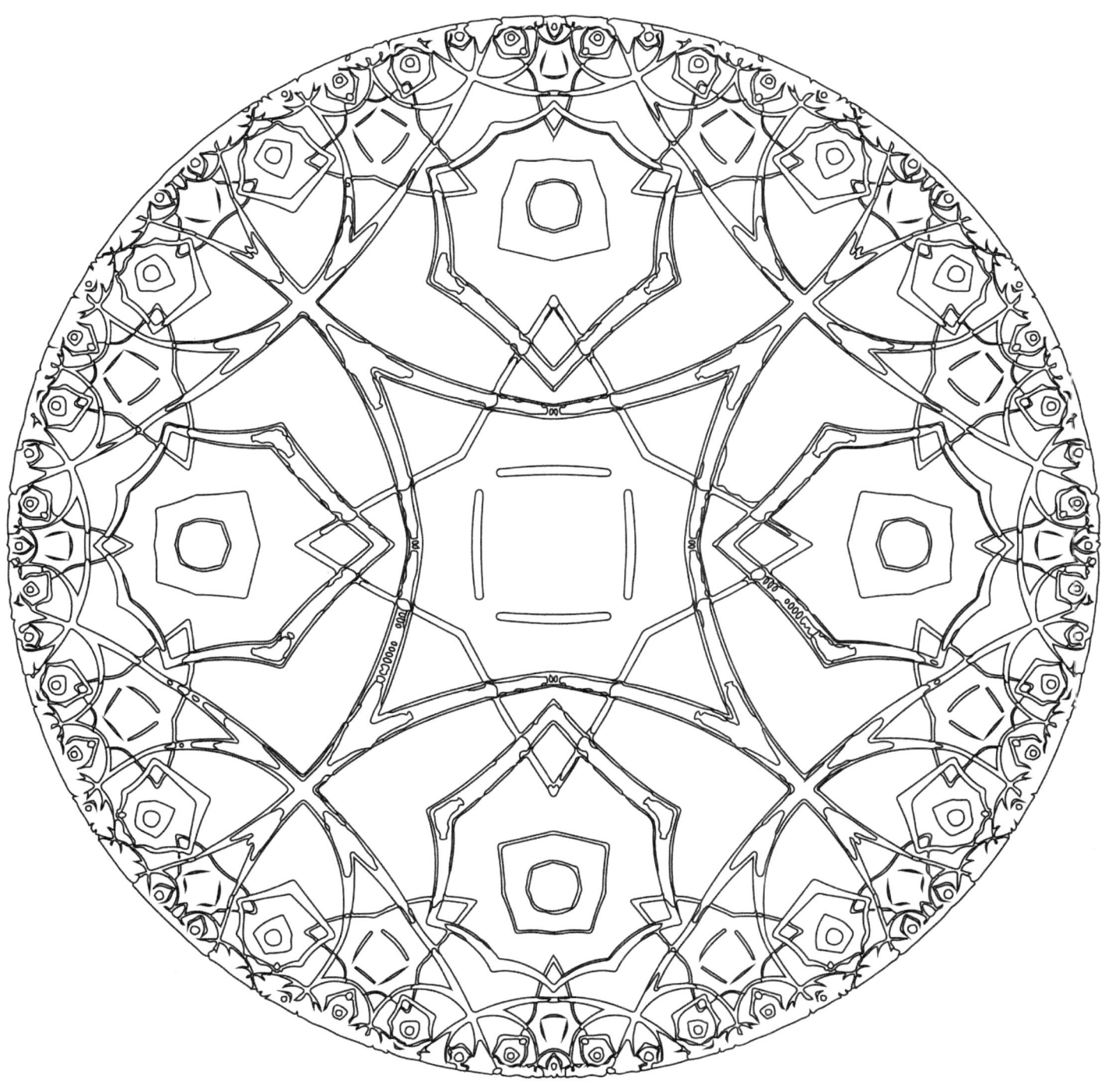

Activity 96: Falling leaves

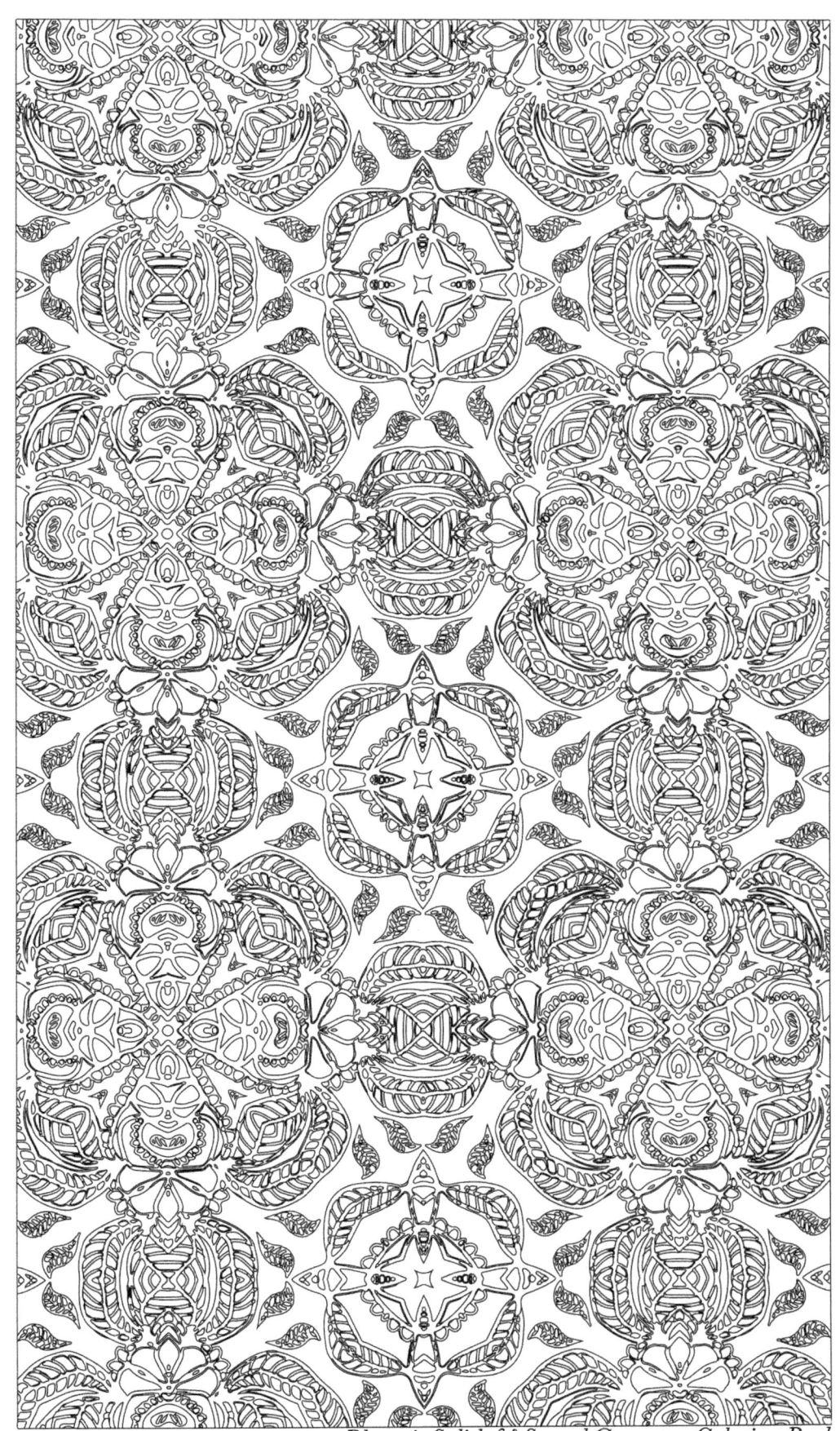

Activity 97: Polygon

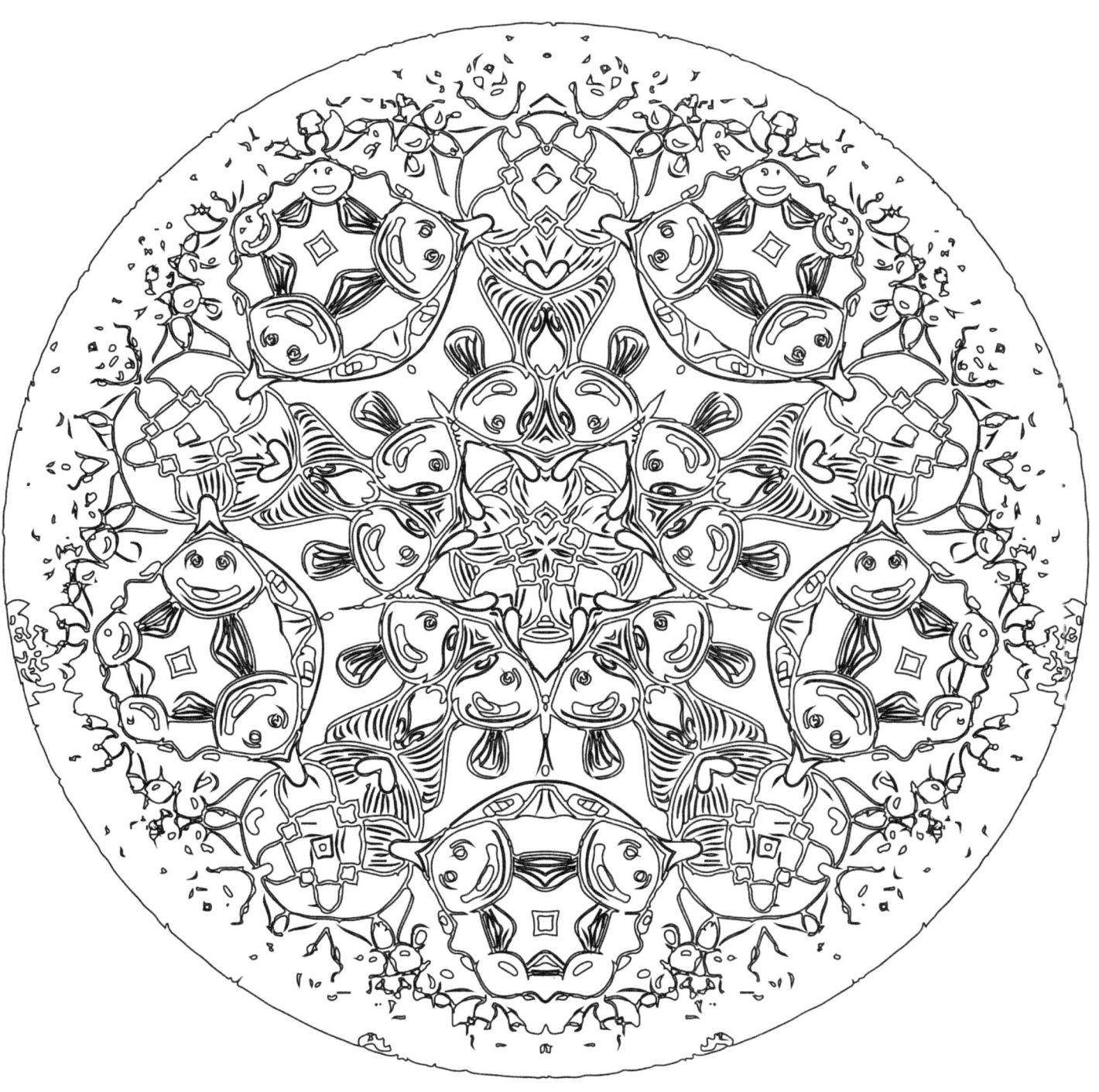

Activity 98: Endogendo

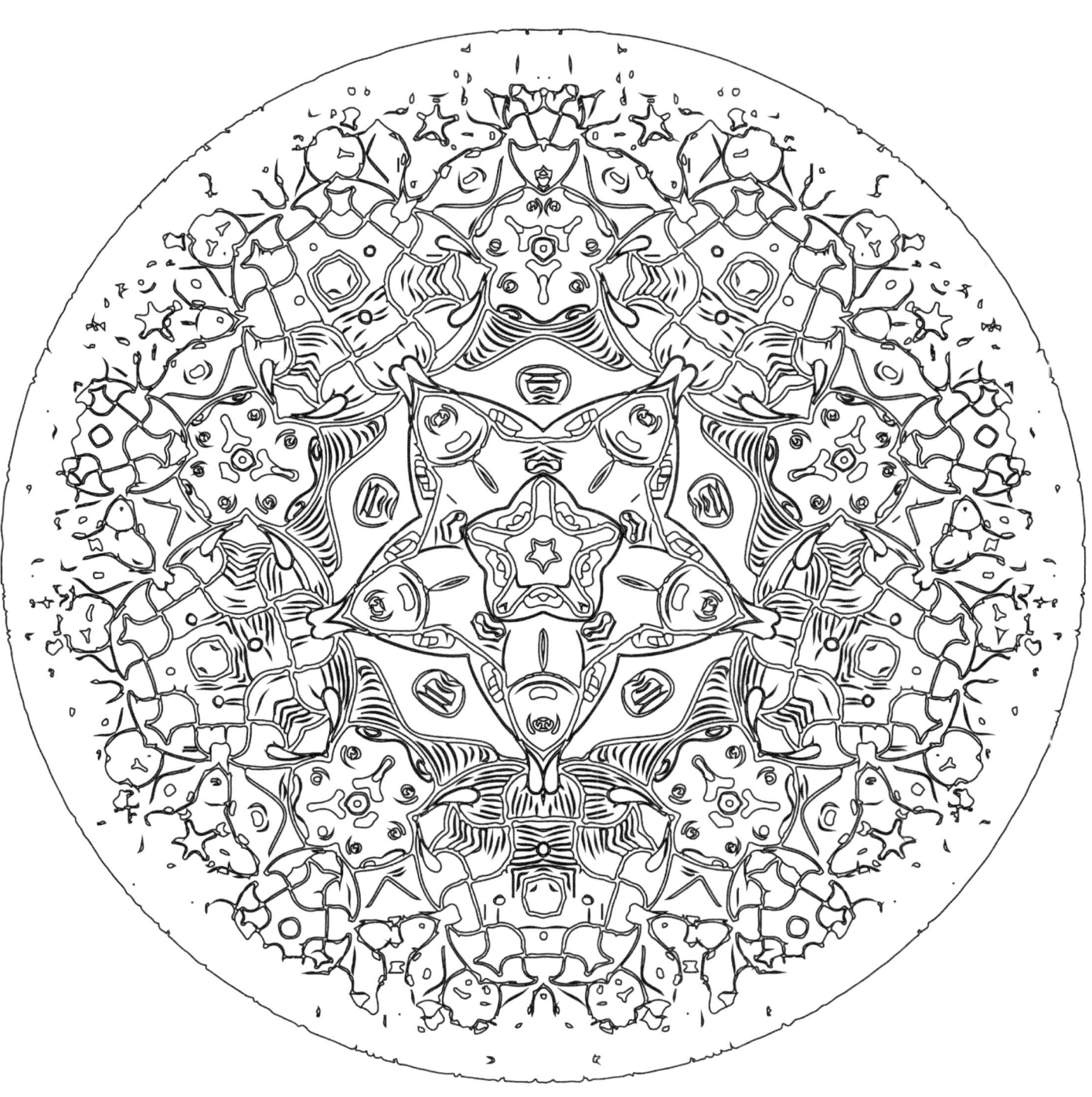

Activity 99: Sacred leaves

Activity 100: Bells

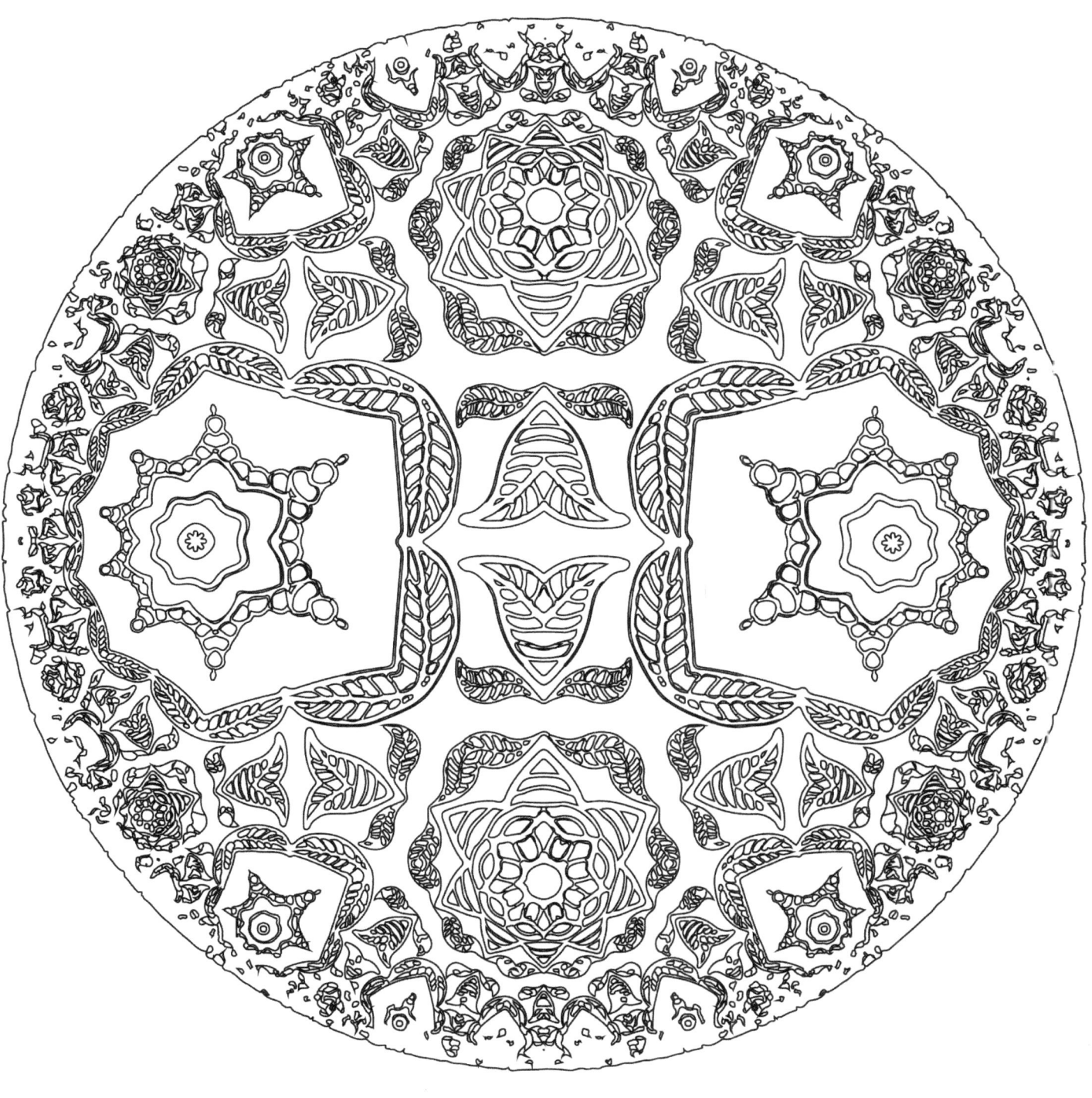

Activity 101: Nebula

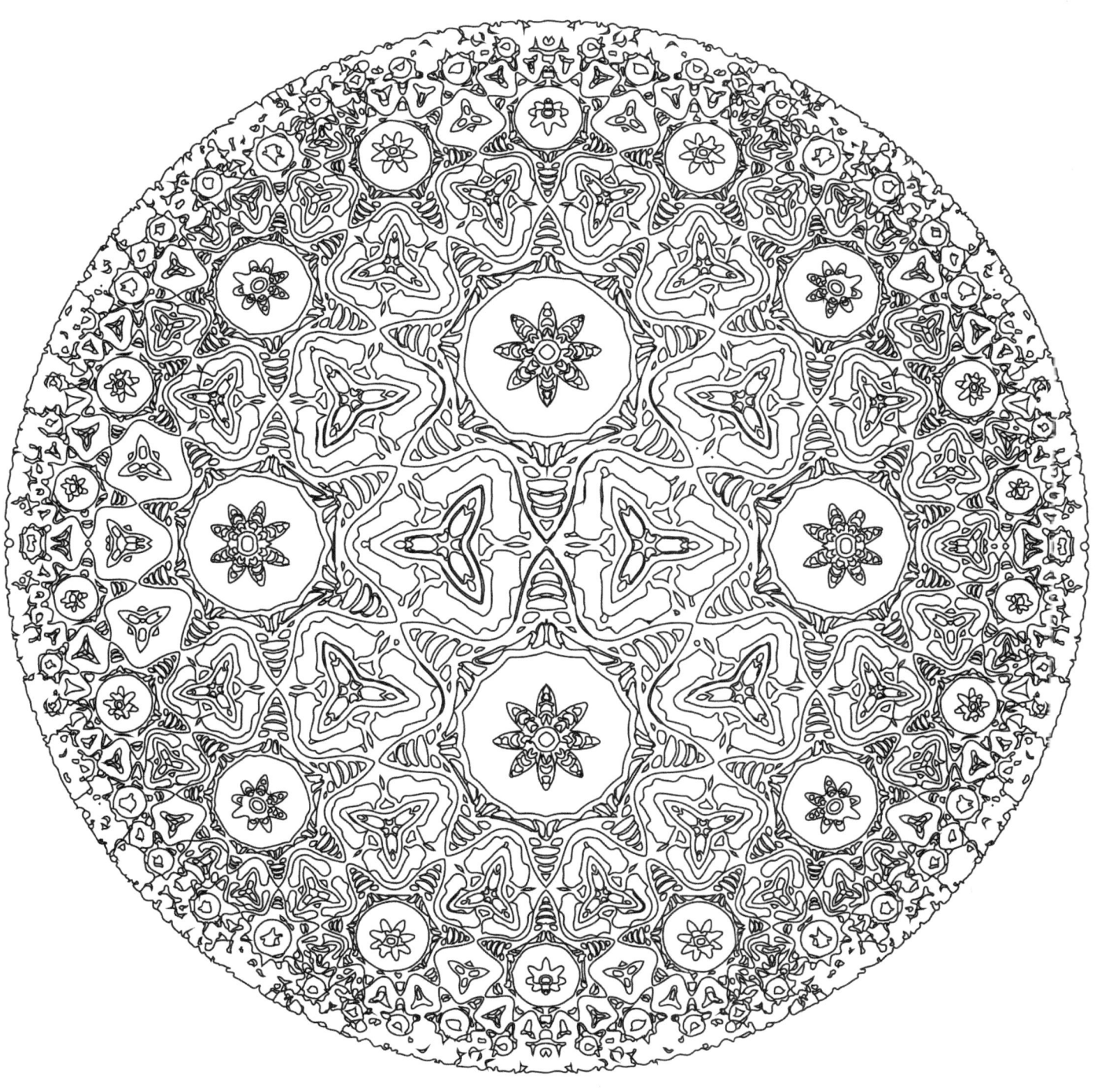

Acknowledgement

Floral background design created by Visnezh - Freepik.com.
Some designs created using http://weavesilk.com

"The Secret of the Temple, Earth Energies, Sacred Geometry and the Lost Keys of Freemasonry", John Michael Greer, published 2016.

"Sacred Mathematics - Japanese Temple Geometry", Fukagawa Hidetoshi, Tony Rothman. Princeton University Press, published 2008.

www.ingramcontent.com/pod-product-compliance
Lightning Source LLC
Chambersburg PA
CBHW062102220526
45471CB00010B/3577